·8 0· G R E A T
N A T U R A L
S H A D E
G A R D E N
P L A N T S

·80· GREAT NATURAL SHADE GARDEN PLANTS

KEN DRUSE

CLARKSON POTTER/PUBLISHERS
NEW YORK

Published by Clarkson N. Potter, Inc., 201 East 50th Street, New York, New York 10022. Member of the Crown Publishing Group.

Random House, Inc. New York, Toronto, London, Sydney, Auckland

http://www.randomhouse.com/

The photographs in this book were previously published in *The National Shade Garden* by Ken Druse.

CLARKSON POTTER, POTTER, and colophon are trademarks of Crown Publishers, Inc.

Printed in Hong Kong

Library of Congress Cataloging-in-Publication Data is available upon request.

ISBN 0-609-80043-4

10 9 8 7 6 5 4 3 2 1

First Edition

Acknowledgments

I want to thank some of the people who helped produce this book: Chip Gibson, President and Publisher of Crown Publishers; Lauren Shakely, Clarkson Potter's Editorial Director, who suggested this project and made this idea into reality; Maggie Hinders, the book designer, whose contribution is obvious; Lisa Sloane, who assisted with design; and Mark McCauslin, production editor, and Joan Denman, production manager. Their less visible work was equally important.

I want to thank Laurie Stark, Joan De Mayo, Tina Constable, and Mary Ellen Briggs for always doing more than their share on our projects. I am especially grateful to my editor, Eliza Scott. Thanks also to Helen Pratt, my indefatigable agent; Louis Bauer for his patience; and George Waffle for his friendship and efforts. I also must thank Ruth Clausen, whose help in making this book accurate and useful was invaluable.

Lastly, I have to thank you. As I travel and lecture around the country, it is so gratifying to learn that my books have helped (and touched) so many.

The plants I've chosen are presented with their cousins and intimate friends from the botanical community—in all, hundreds to collect and grow.

Contents

Introduction

Every gardener has shade. If you have only a single tree, then you garden in its shadow. Neighboring buildings cast shade onto urban gardens and the suburban house blocks the morning sun on the west side, afternoon sun on the east side, and nearly all the sunlight on its north side. Years ago, I talked to gardeners about their number one lament—too much shade. "Could I cut down my neighbor's tree?" they would ask. That changed, however, within a few years of the publication of *The Natural Shade Garden,* in 1992, which I wrote because I found myself plunged into the relative darkness of a 20 × 50-foot backyard garden in Brooklyn, New York. My discoveries changed the way I view shade. I love gardening here now, in this most gentle atmosphere where the dense plants shade out most weeds, and the humus-rich woodland soil holds moisture, reducing watering chores.

Today, shade gardening is a fast-growing aspect of America's most popular outdoor leisure-time activity. Now, as I travel around the country, I am not surprised to hear the question, "How can I make more shade?" There are several reasons for this radical change. We have learned that for our health, it is not such a good idea to be out in the full sun in the middle of the day. And who wants to suffer in the heat of the sunny garden when you can bask in the cool places loved by the shadowed plantings? But gardeners also began to realize that the shady condition was not a curse but an opportunity to develop new places around their properties—places they thought could not be cultivated at all. Suddenly, some of the most spectacular members of the plant kingdom were welcome in their gardens.

The American native plant movement began with a love for the exquisite woodland wildflowers such as trillium, bloodroot, Virginia bluebells, and shooting star, and a concern for their preservation. These wild plants and their cousins from the temperate forests of the world make up the residents of our sheltered gardens.

The gardens that I love are informally designed and owe more to wild America than to traditional garden styles like French parterres or the intricately clipped trees and shrubs of the Japanese model. I call them natural gardens, not just because they take their inspiration from the wild, but also because we are asking nature to become an equal partner in the vitality and maintenance of the garden. These are earth-friendly places and there are several steps toward reaching this happy state. Soil must be well prepared, air circulation unimpeded, moisture available, and so on. We search for the best ways to avoid problems and, if they occur, select the most organic, benign means of dealing with them. If insects appear on a shrub, our first line of defense is to try a spray of plain water from the hose to dislodge as many as possible. If that doesn't work, we turn to modern remedies such as the fatty acids—soaps—curatives that kill harmful insects but usually do not harm beneficial ones such as lady bugs and bumble bees. These soaps are generally not as effective as the chemical arsenals available a decade ago, but that's all right. I can endure an occasional hole in a leaf for our planet's health.

The best thing to do is to not challenge nature in the first place. For example, if you plant a young shrub whose tendency is to grow tall next to the house, it may grow to block the view from a window. Conventional garden practice suggests pruning—natural gardening suggests planting a low-growing shrub in the first place. And in the case of shade, that means planning with this situation in mind. If

you put a sun-loving perennial in the shade, it will stretch for the light, becoming spindly, weak, and prey to disease and pests. The converse situation is true, of course; the shade plant burns to a crisp in the sun. Understanding this simple premise—the right plant for the right place—will begin to unlock the rich knowledge about your garden and the best way to play your role.

Selecting the right plant is only one step. A new saying, "Don't fight the site," goes beyond plant selection. Take an inventory of the conditions around your property and even the specific spots within the shade garden. What causes the shade? Are there roots from trees that will compete with plants you hope to install? Is your site moist or dry? Is the soil rich or poor? If your site is moist, find plants that like wet feet. Soil can be and, in many cases, should be amended with compost or manure to boost nutrition for a plant that likes that, or left lean for ones that prefer a poor soil. But keep in mind some of the big-picture items and, instead of altering them, consider accepting them. If nature hands you a pile of rocks, make a rock garden. In the past, that rock pile would have been blasted with dynamite for a swimming pool, and perhaps the woodland that makes our shade garden would have been cleared for lawn.

Today, these ideas are not as radical as they were when I

proposed them in 1989's *The Natural Garden.* That book defined what might be considered an American garden style. Gardeners have embraced *The Natural Shade Garden,* as well, and wherever I go, someone will come up to me clutching that book and tell me it is his or her "bible." Now a popular question is, "What are some of the best plants to grow in the shade?"

This book presents 80 great shade garden plants and talks about hundreds of related varieties and species along with companion plants to grow along with the selections. The accompanying text presents the needs for each plant: its climate zones, soil and moisture requirements, flower color or height at maturity. I've thrown in a pronunciation guide since it may be a bit hard to figure out how to say the Latin name. But this generic name is important to learn, helping you to make sure you are buying the exact plant you want. Common names may be regional or colloquial at best, but if you learn its Latin name, you will begin to treat the plant as an individual. That is another step to great gardening—to realize that knowing your plants as unique entities with specific requirements helps in placement and self-sufficiency—nature's role in the garden again.

Take this book with you to the nursery and, please, out to the garden, as well.

Ornamental Shrubs

Ornamental Shrubs

We often hear about the bones of a garden—its overall design viewed best in winter, when walls, paving, and other permanent elements are easy to see. But I think shrubs provide much of the structure in natural, informal gardens in the shade. These woody plants with multiple stems emanating from or near the ground can be deciduous or evergreen. Some grow a few inches tall, while others reach up to a second-story window. All bloom by species or variety, with flowers in nearly every color and size—ranging from the barely visible, apricot-scented sweet olive (*Osmanthus fragrans*) to *Hydrangea macrophylla* umbels as large as a baby's head. In the forest, shrubs inhabit the understory, presenting a transitional layer between the treetop canopy and the woodland floor. They perform similarly in our gardens by softening the hard forms of tree trunks and buildings, becoming foils for our herbaceous plantings, and defining spaces with living "walls." Shrubs make the framework from which we hang many of our other horticulture accoutrements.

The most popular shrub for shade is *Rhododendron;* however, this is not just one plant. It is a genus with literally thousands of evergreen, deciduous, tiny to huge shrubs with flowers in all colors but true blue and black. Most blossom in mid- to late spring; but a few, *R. prunifolium,* for example, bloom as late as early fall. Of course people do not garden by one genus alone (although *Rhododendron* collectors might like to believe otherwise).

Select some flowers that bloom from winter to fall: In the South, camellias begin in December; Asian witch hazels have fragrant ribbonlike flowers in winter; *Corylopsis* spp. present long chains of pale yellow flowers; early viburnums are often intensely fragrant; the double-flowered *Kerria japonica* 'Pleniflora' has Kodak-yellow pompons when daffodils bloom; *Deutzia* spp. have delicate white flowers in profusion. *Calycanthus floridus* is Carolina sweet shrub, with brownish red flowers and a haunting fragrance; *Hibiscus syriacus,* the rose of Sharon, produces flowers reminiscent of its tropical cousins; just as the Asian witch hazels are among the first to bloom, the autumn-blooming American *Hamamelis virginiana* is the last.

Acer japonicum 'Aureum'
(golden full moon maple)

Aucuba japonica hybrids
(Japanese aucuba)

Clethra alnifolia 'Rosea'
(summersweet)

RIGHT
Camellia japonica hybrids
(Japanese camellia)

ACER JAPONICUM 'AUREUM' [*A. shirasawanum* 'Aureum']

PRONUNCIATION: A-ser ja-PON-i-kum

COMMON NAME: Golden full moon maple

HOMELAND: Japan

HARDINESS: USDA Zones 5—8

SIZE: 10'—20' tall; 10'—20' wide

INTEREST: Golden foliage; flowers in spring

LIGHT CONDITIONS: Light dappled shade

SOIL/MOISTURE: Moist soil, high in organic matter. Should not be allowed to dry out.

DESCRIPTION: There are several cultivars of this species, with varying leaf shapes. 'Aconitifolium' and 'Vitifolium' have superior fall color. Golden full moon maple is a slow-growing, understory plant; in the fall its golden foliage takes on red-orange tints. It effectively lights up shaded areas and looks particularly attractive underplanted with ferns and yellow-flowering perennials such as Welsh poppy (*Meconopsis cambrica*) or *Corydalis lutea*, both of which grow well under the same conditions and bloom for a good part of the season. It is also striking with yellow-variegated hostas such as 'Frances Williams' and 'Gold Standard'. Pruning is minimal and should be confined to gently shaping the plant when young and subsequently removing any damaged or dead branches. Pests and diseases are seldom a problem.

AUCUBA JAPONICA HYBRIDS

PRONUNCIATION: a-KEW-ba ja-PON-ik-a

COMMON NAME: Japanese aucuba

HOMELAND: Japan; most aucubas on the market are hybrids of garden origin.

HARDINESS: USDA Zones 7—10

SIZE: 6'—10' tall; 5'—6' wide

INTEREST: Male and female flowers, on separate plants, appear in spring, followed by berries on the females, which turn bright red and remain through the winter.

LIGHT CONDITIONS: Light to heavy shade

SOIL/MOISTURE: Well-drained, moist soil, high in organic matter. Tolerates heavy, even compacted soils.

DESCRIPTION: The Japanese aucuba hybrids are valuable small shrubs whose evergreen leaves, often dappled with gold as in 'Variegata' (female) and 'Mr. Goldstrike' (male), enliven shaded places. For berry production, a male must be planted alongside or close to female specimens. These tough plants tolerate the shade cast by beeches, horse chestnuts, and other deciduous trees, but they must remain shaded from intense sun during the winter months to avoid sunburn. There are dwarf clones available such as 'Nana Variegata', which remains about half the full size. 'Serratifolia' has coarsely toothed leaf margins; 'Sulphurea' has dark green leaves tinged gold along.

CAMELLIA JAPONICA HYBRIDS

PRONUNCIATION: ka-MEL-ia ja-PON-ik-a

COMMON NAME: Japanese camellia

HOMELAND: China, Japan, but hybrids are of garden origin

HARDINESS: USDA Zones 7–10

SIZE: 10'–15' tall; 6'–10' wide

INTEREST: Late winter to spring, with single or double rose-like flowers in white, pinks, and reds, some variegated

LIGHT CONDITIONS: Light dappled shade, especially in winter to avoid leaf burn

SOIL/MOISTURE: Well-drained, acid soil, amended with plenty of organic matter to retain moisture. Water deeply during dry weather, as drying out often promotes flower bud drop.

RELATED SPECIES: Sasanqua camellia (*C. sasanqua*) has smaller leaves and flowers.

DESCRIPTION: The numerous Japanese camellia hybrids are valued as much for their glossy evergreen foliage as for their showy waxy flowers during the dark days of the year. The most popular are early-flowering 'Debutante', double light pink; late-blooming 'Kumasaka', semi-double dark pink; and midseason 'Kramer's Supreme', with fragrant, peony-shaped, brilliant red frilled flowers. In northern climes, camellias are frequently grown in sunrooms and conservatories.

CLETHRA ALNIFOLIA 'ROSEA'

PRONUNCIATION: KLETH-ra al-ni-FOE-lee-a

COMMON NAME: Summersweet

HOMELAND: Native; Maine to Florida; cultivar of garden origin

HARDINESS: USDA Zones 3–9

SIZE: 3'–8' tall and almost as wide

INTEREST: Glossy dark green foliage that turns vivid yellow in fall. Spires of small, sweet-smelling, pinkish (white in the species) flowers in late summer.

LIGHT CONDITIONS: Partial shade to full sun

SOIL/MOISTURE: Moisture-retentive, acid soil, amended with compost or leaf mold

DESCRIPTION: This beautiful native deserves a place in even small gardens. In late summer, when few shrubs are in bloom, the fragrance of summersweet is overwhelming and attracts bees and butterflies in droves. It does well beside ponds and lakes and also tolerates seaside conditions. Combine it with swamp rose mallow (*Hibiscus moscheutos*), or plant it in a shrub collection with *Calycanthus floridus*. The flowers are borne on young wood, so prune in winter or early spring. There are several other notable cultivars, including 'Hummingbird', a 4'-tall shrub with white flowers, and shell pink 'Pink Spires'. Both are fragrant.

Deutzia gracilis
(slender deutzia)

Hydrangea quercifolia
(oakleaf hydrangea)

Kerria japonica
(Japanese kerria)

LEFT
Enkianthus campanulatus
(redvein enkianthus)

DEUTZIA GRACILIS

PRONUNCIATION: **DOOT-see-a GRAS-i-lis**
COMMON NAME: **Slender deutzia**
HOMELAND: **Japan**
HARDINESS: **USDA Zones 5–8**
SIZE: **2'–4' tall, sometimes to 6'; 3'–4' across**

INTEREST: **Panicles of pure white, ½"–¾" flowers in spring**
LIGHT CONDITIONS: **Best in very light shade**
SOIL/MOISTURE: **Well-drained soil of average fertility**

DESCRIPTION: Slow-growing slender deutzia is reliably beautiful in bloom but is less interesting during other seasons. It is best massed or used as a dense but graceful filler in shrub borders; in mixed borders it combines well with perennials and adds structure, but where space is limited this shrub may earn its keep only for a few weeks in spring. Prune routinely after flowering; cut back hard to within a few inches of the ground if the plant becomes unshapely. Dead wood may be removed at any time. *D.* × *rosea* and its cultivar 'Carminea' have pink flowers. *D. gracilis* (*D. crenata*) 'Nikko' has masses of double flowers on low, spreading plants. In fall the bright green foliage turns deep burgundy. Excellent as a ground cover in sun or light shade. Pest and disease free.

ENKIANTHUS CAMPANULATUS

PRONUNCIATION: **en-kee-AN-thus kam-pan-u-LA-tus**
COMMON NAME: **Redvein enkianthus**
HOMELAND: **Japan; there are several good named forms on the market.**
HARDINESS: **USDA Zones 5–9**
SIZE: **Seldom more than 8' tall in north, but to 15' elsewhere; upright, 4' or so across**
INTEREST: **Blooms in spring with nodding clusters of cream bells, delicately veined with coral red. Foliage turns brilliant red, orange, and yellow in fall.**
LIGHT CONDITIONS: **An understory shrub for partial shade**
SOIL/MOISTURE: **Moisture-retentive, acid soil, with copious amounts of organic matter**
CULTIVARS: **The popular cultivar 'Red Bells' has redder flowers on a smaller plant.**

DESCRIPTION: Redvein enkianthus is one of the most beautiful shrubs for partly shaded sites. It tolerates city conditions and also adapts to container culture. Underused, it deserves to be planted where its spectacular fall color can be appreciated. It is an excellent companion for other lovers of acid soils such as rhododendrons and azaleas. Carpet its feet with primulas, sweet woodruff, epimediums, or low ferns.

HYDRANGEA QUERCIFOLIA

PRONUNCIATION: hi-DRAN-jee-a kwer-si-FOE-lee-a

COMMON NAME: Oakleaf hydrangea

HOMELAND: Native; Georgia, Mississippi, and Florida

HARDINESS: USDA Zones 5–9

SIZE: 4'–6' tall; 6'–8' wide

INTEREST: In early summer, honey-fragrant white flowers, which mature to blush then to purplish pink and rust, in huge cone-shaped inflorescences, up to 15" long. In fall, the foliage turns to purple and bronze, remaining that way during mild winters. Exfoliating bark.

LIGHT CONDITIONS: Light to dappled shade

SOIL/MOISTURE: Well-drained, humusy soil, amended with organic matter. Keep moist during hot periods and in sun.

CULTIVARS: Several superior selections include 'Snow Queen', without more sterile flowers; 'Alice', a strong grower, to 10' tall; and double 'Snowflake'.

DESCRIPTION: Oakleaf hydrangea is one of our best native shrubs for all seasons—perhaps at its best massed in light woodlands or in shaded shrub collections fronted by hostas or astilbes, especially white-flowering cultivars, low-growing ferns such as Japanese painted fern (*Athyrium nipponicum* 'Pictum'), with drifts of early narcissus to extend the floral display.

KERRIA JAPONICA

PRONUNCIATION: KER-ee-a ja-PON-i-ka

COMMON NAME: Japanese kerria

HOMELAND: Central and western China

HARDINESS: USDA Zones 5–9

SIZE: 3'–6' tall; spreading 6' or more across

INTEREST: In spring, elegant, single 1½" flowers of vivid butter yellow are borne on gracefully arching evergreen stems, clothed with fine-textured, bright green deciduous foliage.

LIGHT CONDITIONS: Tolerates all but deepest shade; blooms best in dappled conditions.

SOIL/MOISTURE: Average well-drained soil. Avoid rich, damp soils.

CULTIVARS: Repeat-blooming, double-flowered 'Pleniflora' has Kodak-yellow pompoms that hold their color well, but growth tends to be loose and ungainly. 'Picta' is an excellent foliage shrub with white-edged leaves that make an impact all season; it bears single yellow flowers.

DESCRIPTION: Kerria suckers freely and makes a dense, rounded shrub. Prune out dead stems routinely. Useful on the edge of woodlands or against walls, where the emerald stems stand out in winter. Combines well with tall perennials such as goatsbeard (*Aruncus dioicus*), daylilies (*Hemerocallis*), and *Ligularia*. Underplant with winter aconite (*Eranthis hyemalis*) for early-spring color.

Leucothoe fontanesiana
(drooping leucothoe,
fetterbush)

Rhododendron prunifolium
(plum-leaved azalea)

Rhus typhina
(staghorn sumac)

Pieris japonica
'Variegata' (variegated
Japanese pieris)

26   80 GREAT NATURAL SHADE GARDEN PLANTS

LEUCOTHOE FONTANESIANA

PRONUNCIATION: lu-KOTH-o-ee fon-ta-nee-zee-A-na

COMMON NAME: Drooping leucothoe

HOMELAND: Native; mountains of Virginia to Georgia and Tennessee

HARDINESS: USDA Zones 4–8

SIZE: 3'–6' tall and wide

INTEREST: This evergreen shrub has a graceful fountain-shaped habit with pointed, lance-shaped leaves. In spring, white lily-of-the-valley-like flowers in dangling clusters.

LIGHT CONDITIONS: Partial to full shade

SOIL/MOISTURE: Well-drained, acid soil, with organic matter to retain moisture

DESCRIPTION: Excellent as a tall ground cover under light woodland and with rhododendrons and azaleas. Site so that the drooping habit shows, such as tumbling over a wall or a large rock outcropping. In the North, winter burn often results in the old leaves becoming unsightly before new growth comes; avoid exposed positions. Stress caused by drought makes the plants more prone to pests and diseases. Cultivars include: 'Girard's Rainbow' (a.k.a. 'Rainbow') has striking new growth streaked with cream and copper, which regrettably turns green with age. 'Scarletta' is a compact form with lustrous purple-red new growth.

PIERIS JAPONICA 'VARIEGATA'

PRONUNCIATION: pi-AIR-is ja-PON-ik-a

COMMON NAME: Variegated Japanese pieris

HOMELAND: Japan; cultivar of garden origin

HARDINESS: USDA Zones 5–8

SIZE: 10'–12' tall; 6'–8' across

INTEREST: Beautiful evergreen foliage, dark green, edged with clean white. Drooping clus-

ters of cream lily-of-the-valley flowers in spring; winter flower buds are also interesting.

LIGHT CONDITIONS: Light dappled shade to open woodland

SOIL/MOISTURE: Well-drained, fertile soil, amended with leaf mold or compost

DESCRIPTION: Japanese pieris is a superior shrub, but in its variegated form it is superb. It grows fairly slowly and fits into small residential gardens with ease. Use as a specimen plant, perhaps in the ell of a building or as a focal point for a group of shrubs. It also tolerates container culture, and can dress up a terrace or rooftop for a whole year. Shelter from the wind and be alert for lace bug damage. There are numerous other cultivars. One of the few deer-proof evergreens.

RHODODENDRON PRUNIFOLIUM

PRONUNCIATION: roe-doe-DEN-dron PRUNE-i-foe-lee-um

COMMON NAME: Plum-leaved azalea

HOMELAND: Native; southwestern Georgia and eastern Alabama

HARDINESS: USDA Zones 5–9

SIZE: 8'–10' tall and almost as wide

INTEREST: In mid- to late summer, clusters of striking orange-red, funnel-shaped flowers burst into bloom.

LIGHT CONDITIONS: Partial to light dappled shade

SOIL/MOISTURE: Moisture-retentive, acid soil

DESCRIPTION: This, among the last of the native rhododendrons to bloom, makes a vibrant splash in the landscape. Prominent, exserted stamens animate the flower show. Best planted in informal settings, along woodland paths, or in open clearings; also mixes well with other shrubs in borders or can be treated as a specimen plant. Underplant with spring-blooming Solomon's seal, lily-of-the-valley, or primroses to extend the season of interest.

RHUS TYPHINA

PRONUNCIATION: ROOS tie-FIN-a

COMMON NAME: Staghorn sumac

HOMELAND: Southeastern Canada, south to Georgia, Indiana, and Iowa

HARDINESS: USDA Zones 3–8

SIZE: 15'–25' tall and as wide from suckers

INTEREST: Deciduous pinnate leaves, which turn brilliant shades of yellow, orange, and red in fall. New growth densely covered with soft hairs. Rusty crimson, fuzzy fruit clusters in fall. Flowers in summer.

LIGHT CONDITIONS: Full sun or light shade

SOIL/MOISTURE: Well-drained, average soil. Tolerates dry, poor soils well.

DESCRIPTION: Staghorn sumac is often found in the wild along rough dry roadsides and railroad tracks and is suitable for large naturalistic settings. It may be used as a huge specimen plant, perhaps in the open as a focal point, or, if space allows, in the ell of a building, where in winter its interesting branching pattern can be seen. Underplant with snowdrops, crocus, and miniature daffodils for spring display. Sometimes an astringent "lemonade" drink is prepared from the fuzzy fruit clusters. Seems to sucker most in cold climates.

Rosa glauca
(redleaf rose)

Skimmia japonica
(Japanese skimmia)

Tsuga canadensis 'Albospica'
(Canadian hemlock)

LEFT
Rubus odoratus
(flowering raspberry,
pink thimbleberry)

ROSA GLAUCA [R. rubrifolia]

PRONUNCIATION: ROE-za GLOW-ka
COMMON NAME: Redleaf rose
HOMELAND: Central and southern Europe
HARDINESS: USDA Zones 2–8
SIZE: 5'–7' tall; spreading 6'–9' across
INTEREST: Purplish red, glaucous leaves, with color best on young growth. Single pink flowers, 1" across, in early summer, followed by hips that persist through the winter.
LIGHT CONDITIONS: Full sun to light shade
SOIL/MOISTURE: Well-drained, fertile soil

DESCRIPTION: This is one rose grown especially for its beautiful foliage. It tolerates more shade than other roses and is suitable for adding to a lightly shaded shrub collection that might include 'Pink Spires' sweet pepperbush. It also combines well with goat's rue, purple coneflowers, pink gladioli, and other perennials and annuals in mixed borders. An interesting backdrop for pink Japanese anemones. Some people hate the little pink "dog" roses. I don't. The burnt-orange, urn-shaped hips that follow are a harmonious accent.

RUBUS ODORATUS

PRONUNCIATION: ROO-bus oh-dor-AH-tus
COMMON NAME: Flowering raspberry, pink thimbleberry
HOMELAND: Native; Nova Scotia to Georgia
HARDINESS: USDA Zones 2–8
SIZE: 6'–9' tall; 6' or so wide
INTEREST: Deciduous shrub with almost thorn-free stems, clothed with felted, maplelike leaves. Fragrant, purplish pink 2" flowers in early summer. Some fall color, and red fruits.
LIGHT CONDITIONS: Light to partial shade
SOIL/MOISTURE: Well-drained, rich soil

DESCRIPTION: It is easy to recognize flowering raspberries as cousins of the rose when single flowers appear. Although not widely grown, flowering raspberries are useful planted with other shrubs, in lightly shaded spots. They grow vigorously and make dense barriers. Prune out old canes in early spring. Provides food and good cover for birds and wildlife. A wonderful, underused native.

SKIMMIA JAPONICA

PRONUNCIATION: SKIM-ee-a ja-PON-i-ka
COMMON NAME: Japanese skimmia
HOMELAND: Japan
HARDINESS: USDA Zones 7–9
SIZE: 3'–4' tall and about as wide
INTEREST: In spring, attractive clusters of small yellowish white flowers bloom; the males are showier. If pollinated, the flowers give way to persistent, shiny scarlet berries on female plants in fall.
LIGHT CONDITIONS: Partial to full shade. Protect from winter sun.
SOIL/MOISTURE: Moist, acid soil amended with plenty of compost or leaf mold

DESCRIPTION: This fine evergreen is suitable for foundation plantings and formal parts of the garden. It is excellent in front of larger rhododendrons and azaleas and also does well in containers. For berry production, both male and female plants must be present. *S. reevesiana* is a self-pollinating species.

TSUGA CANADENSIS 'ALBOSPICA'

PRONUNCIATION: SOO-ga ka-na-DEN-sis
COMMON NAME: Canadian hemlock
HOMELAND: Nova Scotia to the mountains of Georgia and Alabama and west to Minnesota; cultivars of garden origin
HARDINESS: USDA Zones 3–8
SIZE: 40'–70' tall; 25' or so wide; some cultivars may be as little as 3' tall and as wide.
INTEREST: Fine evergreen needles and interesting habit; striking new growth
LIGHT CONDITIONS: Tolerates medium to heavy shade well.
SOIL/MOISTURE: Moist, well-drained soil, not strongly alkaline. Amend with compost or leaf mold.

DESCRIPTION: Valuable for hedges, foundation plantings, and woodland plantings and as specimens. 'Albospica' has attractive white tips to the shoots; there are numerous other cultivars differing in height and habit. 'Cole's Prostrate' has a slow creeping habit; 'Jervis' is broadly pyramidal. 'Horsford' has congested growth on a very dwarf shrub; 'Sargentii' is one of the best weeping forms for use as a specimen plant. Be alert to wind damage, pests, and diseases.

Perennials
for Flowers

Perennials for Flowers

We are accustomed to seeing fewer flowers in the shade garden, where foliage shapes, texture, and colors provide interest. But look close up; there is more to see in these places—more intimate than flower gardens in the open. Kneel down and lift the leaves of the wild ginger to find fleeting, inch-long, urn-shaped flowers that may hold greater fascination than in-your-face sunflowers.

That is the way with the woodland flowers—especially the "ephemerals"—plants that sprout and bloom before the leaves on the trees above emerge. These include some of the most outstanding jewels of the botanical kingdom such as trilliums, Virginia bluebells, bright yellow celandine poppy, bloodroot, hepatica, anemones, and spring phloxes. Other plants stick around, offering flower or foliage interest through the summer—such as native bleeding hearts and pulmonarias respectively. Primroses bloom on and off through the growing season by variety, as do the *Cimicifugas,* whose long flower wands end in white pearl buds opening to fluffy fragrant flowers.

Astilbes are ubiquitous perennials for partial shade. They have feathery spikes in colors from red to white, and look best in masses—even used as ground covers. Make a narrow, serpentine planting about 10 feet long using all of a kind, or arrange several colors of a few varieties to flow from pale to deep shades. If the lightest colors are closest with the darkest ones farthest away, the planting will visually elongate the scene. The reverse will foreshorten the view.

One of the longer-blooming cold-hardy perennials is yellow fumatory (*Corydalis lutea*)—a bleeding heart relative with perky yellow flowers from spring to fall. Another perennial that is not hardy outblooms it—impatiens. Tender impatiens may look artificial because they are overused and used badly. You would be hard-pressed to find a natural model for a planting of all-different-color polka-dot impatiens lined in a row. It boils down to the ones you choose and the ways you use them. Plant clusters of one color near patches of another. White ones will light the shadiest place but overpower neighbors. Remember the astilbe model.

Astilbe species (false spirea)

Chasmanthium latifolium (northern sea oats, spangle grass)

Corydalis lutea (yellow fumitory, yellow corydalis)

ASTILBE SPECIES AND CULTIVARS

PRONUNCIATION: as-TIL-bee

COMMON NAME: False spirea

HOMELAND: China and Japan; cultivars of hybrid origin

HARDINESS: USDA Zones 4—9

SIZE: 1′—4′ tall; spreading 1′—3′ across

INTEREST: In summer, fuzzy 6″—18″ spikes of white, pink, lavender, or red flowers rise above handsome fernlike foliage. The leaves of some, especially red cultivars, emerge red in early spring. Ornamental in seed as well as in blooms.

LIGHT CONDITIONS: Light to medium shade, or filtered light

SOIL/MOISTURE: Rich, moist soil, amended with manure, compost, or leaf mold

DESCRIPTION: Most of the astilbes on the market today are grouped under the heading of *A. × arendsii.* 'Bridal Veil', at 2′ tall, and 'Prof. van der Wielan', at 3′, are popular cultivars among the whites. Good pinks include orchid-pink 'Cattleya', which grows 3′ tall, and clear pink 'Rheinland', at 2′. The 2′-tall 'Fanal' has dark bronzy foliage and crimson flowers. A combination of *A. chinensis* 'Pumila' backed by 'Cattleya', with *A. taquetii* 'Superba' behind, makes a stunning scene. Excellent beside ponds, streams, and lakes, all are classic companions for hostas, and good in containers if kept damp.

ASTILBE CHINENSIS 'PUMILA'

PRONUNCIATION: as-TIL-bee chin-EN-sis

COMMON NAME: Chinese astilbe

HOMELAND: China; cultivar of garden origin

HARDINESS: USDA Zones 3—8

SIZE: 12″—18″ tall; spreading to 2′ across

INTEREST: Produces dense spikes of crushed-raspberry-colored flowers in summer; leaves are bronzy and deeply cut.

LIGHT CONDITIONS: Light to medium shade

SOIL/MOISTURE: Moisture-retentive, organic soil, enriched with plenty of manure, compost, or leaf mold. Keep constantly moist.

DESCRIPTION: Although variable in height, 'Pumila' is perhaps the best of the false spireas to use as a ground-cover plant. It spreads readily and effectively chokes out weeds under shrubs and foundation plantings. Allow the spent cinnamon-colored flower spikes to remain on the plants into the winter, for interest during the dark days. Another mini to try is 'Sprite', with airy flowers.

CHASMANTHIUM LATIFOLIUM

PRONUNCIATION: **kas-MAN-thee-um lat-ih-FOL-ee-um**

COMMON NAME: **Northern sea oats, spangle grass**

HOMELAND: **South, central, and eastern North America**

HARDINESS: **USDA Zones 5–9**

SIZE: **2′–3′ tall; 1′ across**

INTEREST: **Light green, grassy leaves that turn copper in fall and brown in winter. Flat flower spikes that brown and persist well into winter. Flowers mid-summer.**

LIGHT CONDITIONS: **Partial shade**

SOIL/MOISTURE: **Moisture-retentive, rich to average soil**

DESCRIPTION: Clump-forming northern sea oats is a beautiful grass over a very long season. Upright in the spring, the foliage mixes well with early perennials; later on, its habit relaxes when it comes into flower, and it takes a more prominent position in the border. A good container plant, and also sought after in the cutting garden. Its tolerance of salty conditions makes it an ideal choice for seaside gardens. Cut down in late winter or early spring; a stand of it is a beautiful sight dusted with winter snow.

CORYDALIS LUTEA

PRONUNCIATION: **kor-RID-al-is LOO-tee-a**

COMMON NAME: **Yellow fumitory, yellow corydalis**

HOMELAND: **Southern Europe**

HARDINESS: **USDA Zones 5–10**

SIZE: **12″–15″ tall and wide**

INTEREST: **Plants produce grayish green foliage, which serves as a perfect foil for the numerous clusters of small, bright yellow, snapdragon-like flowers, which bloom from spring to late summer, even into fall.**

LIGHT CONDITIONS: **Partial shade to shade**

SOIL/MOISTURE: **Well-drained soil of average fertility. Tolerates alkaline soil but not wet feet.**

DESCRIPTION: Owing to its long period of bloom, yellow fumitory is apt to seed itself around all over the place, but seedlings are easy to weed out or welcome because this is a relatively short-lived perennial. The sunny flowers show up well against a background of stone in the rock garden or between paving stones along a path. In shaded borders, pair with blue-green hostas such as 'Big Daddy' and pick up the yellow with hosta 'Frances Williams' or one of the variegated lilyturfs. Also effective growing among *Juniperus procumbens* 'Nana'.

Cyclamen hederifolium
(hardy cyclamen)

Dicentra formosa 'Alba'
(western bleeding heart)

Dicentra spectabilis
(bleeding heart)

LEFT
Cimicifuga racemosa (black
snakeroot, bugbane,
black cohosh)

CIMICIFUGA RACEMOSA

PRONUNCIATION: sim-mee-sif-FYOU-ga ras-em-OH-sa

COMMON NAME: Black snakeroot, bugbane, black cohosh

HOMELAND: Native; New England to Georgia and Tennessee

HARDINESS: USDA Zones 3–9

SIZE: 5′–8′ tall; spreading up to 4′ across

INTEREST: In late summer, elegant branched stems topped with wandlike spikes of fluffy, creamy white flowers. The handsome dark green foliage is biternately compound.

LIGHT CONDITIONS: Light to dappled shade, or bright light

SOIL/MOISTURE: Moisture-retentive, woodsy soil, high in organic content

DESCRIPTION: Plant in drifts to colonize moist woodlands, under high shade. Black snakeroot also makes a bold statement grouped at the back of perennial or mixed borders or planted among shrubs. *C. simplex,* a species from Kamchatka, and its well-known cultivar 'The Pearl' bloom in the fall; they are especially good companions for *Anemone* × *hybrida* 'Honorine Jobert' or 'Whirlwind'. Slow to become established but worth the wait.

CYCLAMEN HEDERIFOLIUM

PRONUNCIATION: SIK-la-men he-de-ri-FOE-le-um

COMMON NAME: Hardy cyclamen

HOMELAND: Southern Europe

HARDINESS: USDA Zones 5–9

SIZE: 4″–6″ tall; 6″ across

INTEREST: Fall-blooming miniature cyclamen

flowers have swept-back petals, in pink and white. The attractive, marbled, ivy-shaped leaves appear after the flowers and persist through the winter.

LIGHT CONDITIONS: Partial shade to shade

SOIL/MOISTURE: Well-drained, organic soil, amended with lime

DESCRIPTION: The hardy cyclamen are enchanting in any garden in late summer and fall. Plant them in drifts at the base of trees or shrubs, each corm about a foot apart; avoid planting too deeply. Mark where they are planted, as the foliage will die back in spring and it is too easy to dig up the corms when over-planting with annuals, such as wax begonias or wishbone flower. Best in cold-winter climates. Endangered in the wild; be **certain** to obtain corms from nursery-propagated (not wild-collected) stock.

DICENTRA FORMOSA 'ALBA'

PRONUNCIATION: dy-SEN-tra for-MOE-sa
COMMON NAME: Western bleeding heart
HOMELAND: British Columbia to central
  California; hybrids and cultivars of garden
  origin
HARDINESS: USDA Zones 3–9
SIZE: 12"–15" tall and wide

INTEREST: Mounds of yellowish green, fernlike
  foliage, above which bloom white (or red or
  pink), narrowly heart-shaped flowers in loose
  clusters. Long blooming if evenings are cool.
  Flowers in spring, sporadically through fall.
LIGHT CONDITIONS: Light shade to shade
SOIL/MOISTURE: Well-drained, organic soil

DESCRIPTION: This beautiful plant and its eastern counterpart, *D. eximia*, or fringed bleeding heart, are almost indistinguishable and have been hybridized to produce many named cultivars attributed to one species or the other. The red- and pink-flowered sorts usually have bluish green foliage, but this is quite variable, as is the degree of dissection. 'Zestful' has rosy pink flowers; 'Silver Smith' has bluish leaves and white flowers. 'Luxuriant' and 'Adrian Bloom' both bear bright red flowers, the former having bluer, more compact foliage.

DICENTRA SPECTABILIS

PRONUNCIATION: dy-SEN-tra spek-TAH-bi-lis
COMMON NAME: Bleeding heart
HOMELAND: Japan
HARDINESS: USDA Zones 2–9
SIZE: 2'–3' tall; spreading about 18" across
INTEREST: Loose mounds of divided leaves. In
  late spring the heart-shaped 1" flowers, pink

or white, are borne along one side of the
gently arching but brittle stems, looking
much like lockets strung in a row.
LIGHT CONDITIONS: Partial shade
SOIL/MOISTURE: Moisture-retentive, organic
  soil, amended with compost or leaf mold

DESCRIPTION: A favorite of gardeners for generations, bleeding heart somehow captures the romance of gardening. In most climates the foliage yellows and dies back after bloom, leaving an awkward hole in the border. Combine with other perennials, especially ferns or hostas, which will grow into the gap. Underplant with spring bulbs, perhaps a pink narcissus such as 'Pink Champion'; *D. s.* 'Alba' looks good with *Narcissus* 'Thalia' or 'Ice Follies'. Bleeding heart may be grown quite successfully in containers, either forced for early bloom indoors or grown naturally outside.

Dodecatheon meadia 'Album'
(shooting star,
American cowslip)

Doronicum caucasicum
(leopard's bane)

Epimedium × *youngianum*
'Niveum' (Young's
barrenwort)

RIGHT
Digitalis purpurea
(common foxglove)

DIGITALIS PURPUREA

PRONUNCIATION: dij-i-TAH-lis pur-pew-REE-a

COMMON NAME: Common foxglove

HOMELAND: Europe

HARDINESS: USDA Zones 4–10

SIZE: 4'–5' tall; 2'–3' wide

INTEREST: Foxgloves have a basal rosette of large, oval, grayish green leaves. In late spring to summer, a single flower stalk bears a one-sided spike of purple, sometimes white, velvety tubular flowers.

LIGHT CONDITIONS: Light to medium shade

SOIL/MOISTURE: Average soil, amended with plenty of manure, compost, or leaf mold to retain moisture

DESCRIPTION: Widely grown as a cottage plant since the Middle Ages, foxgloves go by numerous country names; in Wales they are known as Mary's thimble and are sometimes depicted in stained-glass windows. They are naturally biennial, but in mild regions they may overwinter and rebloom. In any case they self-sow freely, so that after a few seasons they behave as perennials. Several strains such as the Foxy hybrids and Excelsior hybrids have larger flowers, borne all around the stem and held at right angles, revealing speckled interiors. The white 'Alba' is especially showy; avoid cross-pollination with other color forms. Mass or group for best effect. Browse catalogs for unusual species.

DODECATHEON MEADIA 'ALBUM'

PRONUNCIATION: doe-di-CATH-ee-on MEE-dee-a

COMMON NAME: Shooting star; American cowslip

HOMELAND: Native; Pennsylvania to Georgia and west to Texas

HARDINESS: USDA Zones 4–8

SIZE: 1'–2' in bloom; 12" or so across

INTEREST: Basal rosette of pinkish, smooth spatulate leaves. In spring to early summer, a pinkish flower stalk rises and terminates in an umbel of pink or white dart-shaped flowers, each carried on an arching spoke.

LIGHT CONDITIONS: Light woodland shade to shade

SOIL/MOISTURE: Cool, moist but well-drained, woodsy soil

DESCRIPTION: This plant is rare in gardens but native to woodlands and even prairies. 'Album' is a white selection that comes true from seed. It is lovely in light woodland settings grouped among ferns for early-season display or in shaded rock gardens. The foliage dies down in summer in all but the coolest climates. Astilbes are also good companion plants and fill in the gap left behind.

DORONICUM CAUCASICUM [D. orientale]

PRONUNCIATION: doe-RON-i-kum kaw-KAS-i-kum

COMMON NAME: Leopard's bane

HOMELAND: Europe and Asia

HARDINESS: USDA Zones 4–8

SIZE: 12"–24" tall; 12"–15" across

INTEREST: Bright yellow daisylike flowers bloom in spring, over rosettes of bright green foliage, toothed along the edges.

LIGHT CONDITIONS: Partial shade

SOIL/MOISTURE: Moisture-retentive soil of average fertility, amended with plenty of organic matter

DESCRIPTION: Although summer dormant in all but the coolest climates, leopard's bane is still worth growing for its bright spring display. An excellent contrast for narcissus, tulips, and other spring bulbs, both in perennial or mixed beds and as cut flowers. Attractive under trees and shrubs, especially forsythia for a yellow combination. Interplant with hostas, ferns, and other shade lovers to fill the gap later.

EPIMEDIUM × YOUNGIANUM 'NIVEUM'

PRONUNCIATION: ep-ee-MEE-dee-um × yun-gee-AYE-num

COMMON NAME: Young's barrenwort

HOMELAND: Of garden origin

HARDINESS: USDA Zones 5–8

SIZE: 12" tall; 8"–10" across

INTEREST: In spring, small, clean white flowers dance above compound leaves composed of 9 oval or heart-shaped leaflets. These are often rimmed with red when young and turn red and bronze in fall.

LIGHT CONDITIONS: Light shade to shade

SOIL/MOISTURE: Well-drained, organic soil, amended with compost or leaf mold. Tolerates dry shade once established.

DESCRIPTION: Excellent as ground-cover plants, epimediums are all lovely in flower as well as in leaf. Longspur barrenwort (E. grandiflorum) and its white, violet, and pink cultivars have larger flowers and bloom earlier. Yellow-flowered E. pinnatum spp. colchicum is also popular. Useful under shrubs and small trees and at the front of mixed and perennial borders. Cut back to ground level in early spring. Plant with lungworts, Solomon's seal, and fringed bleeding heart for interesting foliage effect. It grows slowly but will spread with the gardener's helpful division.

Erythronium species
(dog's-tooth violet)

Helleborus argutifolius
(Corsican hellebore)

Hosta 'Blue Cadet'
(plantain lily, funkia)

LEFT
Gentiana andrewsii (bottle
or closed gentian)

ERYTHRONIUM SPECIES

PRONUNCIATION: e-rith-ROAN-ee-um
COMMON NAME: Dog's-tooth violet
HOMELAND: Northern U.S., Europe, Asia
HARDINESS: USDA Zones 2–8
SIZE: 6"–24" tall, depending on species; 6"–18" across
INTEREST: Basal rosettes of foliage emerge in early spring and die down after flowering. In some species the leaves are mottled with brown. Nodding lilylike flowers of yellow, purple, or white in spring.
LIGHT CONDITIONS: Light shade to shade
SOIL/MOISTURE: Well-drained, woodsy soil that does not dry out

DESCRIPTION: Dog's-tooth violets are spring ephemerals, ideal in mixed plantings with primroses, lungworts, wood anemones, and trillium in deciduous woodlands, or in naturalistic plantings under shrubs. The eastern native trout lily, *E. americanum,* has yellow flowers on 6" stems and mottled leaves. Californian *E. tuolumnense* has plain leaves and taller yellow flowers; its popular hybrid 'Pagoda' has green wavy leaves and several bright yellow flowers per stem. 'Purple King' has mottled leaves and purple flowers.

GENTIANA ANDREWSII

PRONUNCIATION: jen-chee-AN-a an-DREW-see-eye
COMMON NAME: Bottle or closed gentian
HOMELAND: Quebec to Manitoba, south to New Jersey, and mountains of North Carolina to Missouri
HARDINESS: USDA Zones 3–9
SIZE: 12"–24" tall; about 12" wide
INTEREST: Brilliant blue flask-shaped flowers to 2" long are clustered in the uppermost leaf axils in late summer and fall.
LIGHT CONDITIONS: Partial shade to shade
SOIL/MOISTURE: Moist, rich soil, amended with leaf mold or compost

DESCRIPTION: Although bottle gentian flowers never open, they are prized for their startlingly blue flowers during the waning days of summer. Splendid at water's edge where the blue of Siberian iris stole the show in early summer. Grow them with turtleheads and swamp milkweeds, or with watery-stemmed monkey flowers in yellows and gold. They also thrive in wet woodlands in the company of maidenhair, sensitive, ostrich, and other ferns, but are more tolerant of drier areas than one might imagine. Watch bees crawl inside for nectar.

HELLEBORUS ARGUTIFOLIUS

PRONUNCIATION: hell-e-BORE-us ar-gew-ti-FOE-lee-us

COMMON NAME: Corsican hellebore

HOMELAND: Corsica

HARDINESS: USDA Zones 7–9

SIZE: 18″–24″ tall; up to 36″ across

INTEREST: Heavy clusters of pale green, cupped flowers remain handsome even after petals drop. Evergreen, coarse compound leaves, each toothed along the margins. Flowers late winter to spring.

LIGHT CONDITIONS: Light to moderate shade

SOIL/MOISTURE: Highly organic, well-drained soil, enriched with compost or leaf mold

DESCRIPTION: A bold accent plant in light woodlands; underplant with sweet woodruff or interplant with delicate ferns. In mixed or perennial borders, Corsican hellebore is a fine companion for astilbes, ligularias, corydalis, or hostas. Variegated lungworts and pachysandra are also attractive underplantings and accentuate the apple-green flowers. In the north, try *H. foetidus* for a botanical taste of this plant—it pales, but is an easy-to-grow and rewarding stand-in.

HOSTA 'BLUE CADET'

PRONUNCIATION: HOS-ta

COMMON NAME: Plantain lily, funkia

HOMELAND: Of garden origin

HARDINESS: USDA Zones 3–9

SIZE: 12″–18″ tall in bloom; about 12″ across

INTEREST: Neat clumps of medium-size, heart-shaped, puckered, blue-green leaves and violet-blue, lily-shaped flowers in late summer.

LIGHT CONDITIONS: Tolerates more sun than do many hostas.

SOIL/MOISTURE: Well-drained but moisture-retentive organic soil

DESCRIPTION: Small enough to be grown in the rock garden as a specimen plant or to line a woodland path. Mixes well with other hostas and is valuable planted closely as a ground cover. As with other hostas, be alert for slugs. This is *the* hosta to grow for flowers in a border or the edge of an island bed.

Lamiastrum galeobdolon
[*Lamium galeobdolon*]
'Herman's Pride'
(yellow archangel)

Lathyrus vernus
(spring vetchling or spring
vetch)

Ligularia stenocephala 'The
Rocket' (ligularia, rocket
ligularia)

RIGHT
Impatiens 'Rosette' series
(impatiens, double
impatiens, busy Lizzie)

IMPATIENS 'ROSETTE' SERIES

PRONUNCIATION: im-PAY-shens

COMMON NAME: Impatiens, busy Lizzie

HOMELAND: Of garden origin

HARDINESS: USDA Zones 10–11

SIZE: 6"–18" tall; up to 18" across

INTEREST: Slightly puckered green leaves with clusters of rosebudlike flowers nestling atop each stem from spring to fall.

LIGHT CONDITIONS: Light shade to shade

SOIL/MOISTURE: Well-drained, but moisture-retentive soil of average to rich fertility. They must not dry out.

DESCRIPTION: The species of this tender perennial (*Impatiens wallerana*), treated as an annual in all but the mildest parts of the country, is grown by the acre in public and private gardens nationwide. However, the double-flowered forms have only recently been on the market, and though attractive massed, they deserve to be admired close up in a container, rock garden, or raised bed. Partner with coleus with leaves of a compatible hue, or combine with begonias or caladiums. The compact Rosebud series is easily obtained; variegated-leaved strains are sometimes available.

LAMIASTRUM GALEOBDOLON 'HERMAN'S PRIDE'

PRONUNCIATION: lay-mee-AY-strum ga-lee-OB-do-lon

COMMON NAME: Yellow archangel

HOMELAND: Europe and western Asia; cultivar of garden origin

HARDINESS: USDA Zones 3–9

SIZE: 10"–15" tall; about 18" across

INTEREST: Trailing stems bearing pointed silver and green variegated leaves. Small, hooded yellow flowers cluster in the axils of the upper leaves in late spring.

LIGHT CONDITIONS: Light shade to shade

SOIL/MOISTURE: Average, well-drained but moisture-retentive soil

DESCRIPTION: This low-growing but spreading plant is an ideal choice to front shaded borders that depend on foliage color and texture for their appeal. Plant with white-variegated and plain hostas, variegated pachysandra, and white-variegated ivies, all interspersed with bold-foliaged ferns, ligularias, rodgersias, and darmeras. Although less aggressive than the species, 'Herman's Pride' may also be used as a ground cover; keep it cut back for dense growth and neatness. 'Variegata' is less strongly marked. The vining species is indestructible but will cover an entire area. It is easy to weed out, but might be best grown to spill over the edge of a container.

LATHYRUS VERNUS

PRONUNCIATION: **LATH-i-rus VER-nus**
COMMON NAME: **Spring vetchling, spring vetch**
HOMELAND: **Europe**
HARDINESS: **USDA Zones 4–9**
SIZE: **12″ tall; up to 18″ across**
INTEREST: **Vivid purplish pink flowers in**
spring, which fade to sapphire blue. The shiny foliage, which is summer dormant, consists of 2 or 3 pairs of pointed leaflets.
LIGHT CONDITIONS: **Partial to light shade**
SOIL/MOISTURE: **Average well-drained soil, amended with grit or gravel**

DESCRIPTION: I have seen these underappreciated plants naturalized in a wet woodland clearing under an inch of water. Generally, however, they want excellent drainage to do well. Spring vetchling is suitable for rock gardens or walls, where, once established, its tolerance for drought conditions is an asset. A nice contrast for spring-blooming narcissus, tulips, and other bulbs. 'Roseus' has pink flowers but may be difficult to find; crimson-magenta 'Rose Fairy' is more readily available.

LIGULARIA STENOCEPHALA 'THE ROCKET'

PRONUNCIATION: **lig-yew-LAY-ree-a sten-o-SEPH-a-la**
COMMON NAME: **Ligularia, rocket ligularia**
HOMELAND: **Japan and northern China; cultivar of garden origin**
HARDINESS: **USDA Zones 4–8**
SIZE: **4′ or more tall and almost as wide**
INTEREST: **Clumps of large, jagged-edged,**
deep green leaves are borne on wiry ebony stems. Yellow starry flowers on erect 18″ spikes in summer.
LIGHT CONDITIONS: **Partial shade**
SOIL/MOISTURE: **Well-drained but very moisture-retentive, rich soil, amended with plenty of leaf mold or compost**

DESCRIPTION: Excellent as a foliage plant and equally appealing when in bloom. 'The Rocket' is often listed as a cultivar of *L. przewalskii,* which is similar. Be sure to provide sufficient shade at midday, as the large leaves are prone to unattractive flagging. Not devoured by slugs as are other species. Combine with *Hemerocallis* 'Hyperion' in light shade or large-leafed *Darmera peltata,* a California native, or with ferns and hostas in deeper shade.

Lysimachia ciliata
(fringed loosestrife)

Phlox divaricata (wild sweet
William, woodland phlox)

Scilla siberica
(Siberian squill)

LYSIMACHIA CILIATA

PRONUNCIATION: lie-sim-AK-ia sil-ee-AH-ta
COMMON NAME: Fringed loosestrife
HOMELAND: Quebec to British Columbia, south to Florida, Texas, and Arizona
HARDINESS: USDA Zones 3–9
SIZE: 1'–4' tall; about 2' across

INTEREST: Slender clumps with willowlike leaves, fringed with hairs. Light yellow 1" stars appear in the upper leaf axils. Flowers in mid- to late summer.
LIGHT CONDITIONS: Partial shade
SOIL/MOISTURE: Moist soil preferred

DESCRIPTION: Group at watersides and in other damp places, where their upright habit will contrast with bolder, rounded shapes such as oakleaf hydrangea and *Darmera*. Not as invasive as some other loosestrifes, but be aware of its roving tendencies. 'Purpurea' has deep purplish black young growth; 'Atropurpurea' has bronze-red leaves. These last two are far superior to species as ornamental plants. They spread, too, but all are easy to weed down to the number you want. Pinch growth when about 10 inches tall to encourage stockier plants.

PHLOX DIVARICATA

PRONUNCIATION: FLOKS di-vah-ri-KAH-ta
COMMON NAME: Wild sweet William, woodland phlox
HOMELAND: Native; New England to the southern and south-central states
HARDINESS: USDA Zones 4–9
SIZE: 12"–15" tall; about 12" across

INTEREST: Mats of semievergreen foliage on rooting stems. In mid-spring, light blue or lavender 1½" flower clusters atop 12" stems.
LIGHT CONDITIONS: Light to partial shade
SOIL/MOISTURE: Humus-rich, moist but not waterlogged soil

DESCRIPTION: This attractive woodlander makes a fine edging plant along woodland paths, or a ground cover in informal places. Pure white 'Fuller's White' is more compact; 'Clouds of Perfume' has fragrant, ice blue flowers. 'Louisiana Purple' is taller and bears deep purple flowers. The western *P. d.* var. *laphamii* has darker blue flowers and is probably a parent of the popular maroon-eyed hybrid, *P.* × 'Chattahoochee'. Shear after blooming. The plant is one of the stalwarts of the colorful spring garden.

PRIMULA SPECIES

PRONUNCIATION: **PRIM-yew-la**
COMMON NAME: **Primrose**
HOMELAND: **Asia, Europe, New Zealand, and North America**
HARDINESS: **USDA Zones 3–8**
SIZE: **6″–24″ tall and wide**
INTEREST: **Basal rosettes of crinkly leaves below naked stems topped with solitary or clusters of flowers.**
LIGHT CONDITIONS: **Partial shade suits most.**
SOIL/MOISTURE: **Moist to damp, very rich soil, amended with cow manure, compost, or leaf mold. Most need good drainage.**

DESCRIPTION: This huge genus includes a multitude of garden species, such as English primrose (*P. vulgaris*), cowslip (*P. veris*), and oxlip (*P. elatior*). These have been hybridized to create the polyantha, now called *P.* Pruhonicensis Hybrids. Mass in light woodlands or rock gardens. Plants with red, yellow, pink, blue, or bicolored flowers are offered as pot plants for Mother's Day and can be planted outdoors when the weather warms. The drumstick primrose, *P. denticulata*, has magenta, lavender, or white balls of flowers. Japanese primroses, *P. japonica*, produce tiers of flowers of white, pink, or crimson. They are effective massed with ferns in woodland or waterside settings.

SCILLA SIBERICA

PRONUNCIATION: **SKIL-la sy-BEER-ik-a**
COMMON NAME: **Siberian squill**
HOMELAND: **Central Europe**
HARDINESS: **USDA Zones 2–8**
SIZE: **3″–6″ tall; 3″–4″ across**
INTEREST: **Deep blue flowers, 1–3 per stem, on reddish stems in mid-spring. The straplike leaves may reach 6″ long.**
LIGHT CONDITIONS: **Full sun to medium shade, especially under deciduous trees**
SOIL/MOISTURE: **Well-drained, average soil**

DESCRIPTION: Siberian squills are at their best massed in a naturalistic setting. Plant them by the hundreds if possible, in fall. They are lovely in deciduous woodlands, on dry banks beside ponds or lakes, or as an underplanting for shrubs and foundation plantings. The foliage dies back fairly rapidly after blooming time and should not be removed until it has yellowed. Overplant with annuals, or plant pockets of bulbs between perennials. A perfect companion for other spring-blooming bulbs such as anemones, daffodils, tulips, and hyacinths. 'Spring Beauty' has slightly larger flowers than the species; 'Alba' is white-flowered. Plant with *Chionodoxa* spp., which bloom a bit earlier.

Smilacina racemosa
(false Solomon's seal,
false spikenard)

Stylophorum diphyllum
(celandine poppy)

Viola labradorica
(labrador violet)

RIGHT
Tricyrtis hirta (common
or hairy toadlily)

SMILACINA RACEMOSA

PRONUNCIATION: smy-lass-EE-na ra-say-MOE-sa

COMMON NAME: False Solomon's seal, false spikenard

HOMELAND: Southern Canada and northeast U.S. to Michigan, Tennessee, and Arizona

HARDINESS: USDA Zones 3–9

SIZE: 2'–3' tall; 2'–3' across

INTEREST: Clumps of arching stems that bear broad, lanceolate leaves. The stems terminate in an airy, fragrant, creamy white foamy inflorescence in spring, followed by clusters of round berries.

LIGHT CONDITIONS: Light to dappled shade

SOIL/MOISTURE: Moist, organically rich soil, amended with acid compost or leaf mold

DESCRIPTION: False Solomon's seal is found in the wild in disturbed regions, often beside paths or ditches. It is excellent in transition areas on the edge of woodland, where it provides height to spring plantings. Combine with primulas and forget-me-nots. In early summer the berries turn from green through brownish to red and provide food for wildlife. Its long season of interest makes false Solomon's seal suitable for mixed borders in more formal parts of the garden. Plant the thick rhizomes horizontally. Be alert for slugs.

STYLOPHORUM DIPHYLLUM

PRONUNCIATION: sty-lah-FOR-um dy-FIL-um

COMMON NAME: Celandine poppy

HOMELAND: Native; Pennsylvania to Tennessee, and Wisconsin to Missouri

HARDINESS: USDA Zones 4–9

SIZE: 12"–18" tall; 15"–18" across

INTEREST: Light green, deeply lobed leaves. In spring, large bright yellow poppy flowers to 2" across.

LIGHT CONDITIONS: Partial shade to shade

SOIL/MOISTURE: Woodsy, highly organic soil that retains moisture

DESCRIPTION: Celandine poppy is one of the showiest of our spring ephemerals. It is found in the wild in woodland regions and is displayed at its best in similar places in the garden. Plant with trilliums, Virginia bluebells, and ferns. Unless the soil remains wet, celandine poppies die back when the heat of summer approaches. (But if deadheaded, flowers will form for months.) Allow ferns, astilbes, and hostas to fill the gap. Self-seeds. If transplanting celandine poppies (which they do not relish), take care to avoid damage to the thick, red-sapped rhizomes, which are brittle. The red sap is reminiscent of bloodroot, a close relative. Both were used by Native Americans as dye plants.

TRICYRTIS HIRTA

PRONUNCIATION: tri-SER-tis HIR-ta
COMMON NAME: Common or hairy toadlily
HOMELAND: Japan
HARDINESS: USDA Zones 4–8
SIZE: 2'–3' tall; 12"–15" across
INTEREST: Clumps of arching stems with clasping, softly hairy leaves. In midfall, groups of several purple-spotted white flowers bloom in the upper leaf axils and at the tips of the stems.
LIGHT CONDITIONS: Partial to light shade
SOIL/MOISTURE: Moisture-retentive, deep, rich soil

DESCRIPTION: The curious orchidlike flowers of common toadlilies are best seen up close. They are white, but they are often so spotted and speckled with purple that the overall effect is purple. In the center, the Y-shaped styles are joined to form a spotted, central column. In the perennial or mixed border, site them beside a path, so that they can be observed closely. Self-seeds freely. 'Alba' has pure white flowers and is not quite as robust. Yellow-flowered *T. latifolia* blooms in early summer. In the future, we will have many more species and cultivars from which to choose.

VIOLA LABRADORICA

PRONUNCIATION: VIE-o-la lab-ra-DOE-ri-ka
COMMON NAME: Labrador violet
HOMELAND: Greenland, Canada, and south to Georgia
HARDINESS: USDA Zones 2–8
SIZE: 1"–4" tall; spreading to 12" across
INTEREST: Shallowly toothed, heart-shaped, dark green leaves. Unscented, purple-violet flowers appear mostly in May and sporadically through the season.
LIGHT CONDITIONS: Light or partial shade to shade
SOIL/MOISTURE: Moisture-retentive soil, enriched with compost or leaf mold

DESCRIPTION: Labrador violets are charming additions to rock gardens, beside paths, and in dry-stone walls, as well as part of a mixed woodland carpet. They spread by creeping rhizomes and quickly colonize new areas. 'Purpurea' has darker leaves suffused with purple, especially when young.

Perennials
for Foliage

Perennials
for Foliage

In the shade garden, foliage is king. Just looking at leaves, you will see that perennials for shade are very different from ones for sun. Sun plants have small leaves often covered with hairs, powder, or wax to conserve moisture. They grow on tall stalks arranged in whorls to let in sunlight. Shade perennials usually grow closer to the ground with large leaves that are frequently dark green to absorb more light. They do not need to conserve moisture in the humid woodland environment, so they are thin, smooth, and shiny without protective coatings.

If you can picture painting the sunny border with flowers, then, perhaps, imagine sculpting the shade garden with leaves. At first, don't think about color. Dream of black-and-white forms as you design. Move around these shapes—rearranging them in your mind. Consider the spheres of this plant and columns of that one—for example, a low mound made by the broad, puckered blue leaves of *Hosta seiboldiana* 'Elegans' highlighted by a tall *Astilbe biternata*, a North American native with feathery leaves.

Now you are beginning to focus on the individual shapes of leaves from plants such as *Rodgersia* with large palmate leaves—shaped like giant hands. The Jack-in-the-pulpits have trifoliate leaves, with three parts like the trillium. *Arum italicum* has arrowhead-shaped leaves. *Disporum perfoliatum* looks as if its leaves have been sewn with a zigzag thread, which is actually the stems. *Veratrum* species, or false-hellebores, have huge pleated leaves. From sheets of moss to airy ferns, the variety of foliage shapes and textures seems boundless.

Now add color. *Hostas* in green, gold, or blue, for example. Then there is variegation, when each leaf presents more than one color. Some have outlines that contrast with their centers, or are splashed with white, cream, or gold. I arranged variegated plants in the center of my Brooklyn garden so even on rainy days, or at eight o'clock on a summer night, there seems to be a patch of dappled sunlight on the middle of the garden. You can light up the garden with colorful foliage. Mass, form, texture, shape, and color—these are the media of the shade garden artist.

Adiantum pedatum (northern maidenhair fern)

Coleus × *hybridus*
[*Solenostemon scutellarioides*]
(common coleus)

Helleborus orientalis
(Lenten rose)

RIGHT
Athyrium nipponicum
'Pictum' (Japanese
painted fern)

ADIANTUM PEDATUM

PRONUNCIATION: **ay-dee-AN-tum ped-AH-tum**

COMMON NAME: **Northern maidenhair fern**

HOMELAND: **Native; eastern North America**

HARDINESS: **USDA Zones 2–8**

SIZE: **12″–30″ tall; 12″–15″ across**

INTEREST: **Beautiful, delicate, light green foliage is borne on black stems in palmate whorls like a bird's foot.**

LIGHT CONDITIONS: **Light to medium shade**

SOIL/MOISTURE: **Moist, rich, well-drained woodland soil**

DESCRIPTION: This well-loved and popular clump-forming fern is attractive from when the first fiddleheads unfurl in spring until it gets cut down by cold weather. Its creeping rhizomes are easy to grow. Readily available in the marketplace. Complements woodland plants of all sorts but is especially handsome at the feet of black snakeroot or in combination with larger, less delicate ferns. The leaves always move, even on a still day. This is a real challenge for a photographer, but a gardener will love the way it animates its surroundings.

ATHYRIUM NIPPONICUM 'PICTUM' [*A. goeringianum*]

PRONUNCIATION: **a-THEER-ee-um nip-ON-ik-um**

COMMON NAME: **Japanese painted fern**

HOMELAND: **Eastern Asia**

HARDINESS: **USDA Zones 4–9**

SIZE: **8″–20″ tall; 8″–10″ across**

INTEREST: **Triangular fronds of metallic green are accented along the center with bronze and silver.**

LIGHT CONDITIONS: **Light shade**

SOIL/MOISTURE: **Loose, moist soil, amended with plenty of compost or leaf mold**

DESCRIPTION: Considered by some to be the most beautiful of the ferns for garden culture, Japanese painted fern is pleasing all season long, putting up new fronds into the fall. It is particularly attractive planted as part of a Japanese-style garden, with large rocks and mosses as a foil. Also an interesting partner for similarly colored *Heuchera americana,* which has a quite different leaf form, or cream-variegated hostas. Often planted with astilbes or low azaleas. This is actually one of the easiest ferns to grow.

COLEUS × HYBRIDUS [*Solenosteum scutellaroides*]

PRONUNCIATION: COE-lee-us × HIB-rid-us

COMMON NAME: Common coleus

HOMELAND: Of garden origin

HARDINESS: USDA Zones 10–11

SIZE: 1'–5' tall; about 18" wide

INTEREST: Dramatic foliage in all colors and combinations except blue. The margins of the more-or-less oval leaves are often toothed, frilled, or cut. Spikes of small, brilliant purplish blue flowers in late summer are seldom considered significant.

LIGHT CONDITIONS: Light to partial shade

SOIL/MOISTURE: Well-drained but moisture-retentive soil, with compost or leaf mold

DESCRIPTION: There are many named strains and cultivars of this incredibly diverse group. They are popular for summer bedding in northern climes, where they are treated as annuals. 'Molten Lava' is low growing and has very dark red and carmine leaves; trailing 'Scarlet Poncho', which is useful for hanging baskets, has red leaves trimmed with gold. The chartreuse forms such as 'Pagoda' enliven dark places; their leaf shape contrasts well with *Carex stricta* 'Bowles Golden'. Take cuttings in late summer to root indoors in perlite in a bright window. In three weeks or so, pot the rooted plant. In March, take cuttings from this plant to root and pot for the summer garden and discard the parent.

HELLEBORUS ORIENTALIS

PRONUNCIATION: hell-e-BORE-us o-ree-en-TAL-is

COMMON NAME: Lenten rose

HOMELAND: Greece and Asia Minor

HARDINESS: USDA Zones 4–9

SIZE: 15"–18" tall; 12"–15" across

INTEREST: Evergreen, broadly fingered leaves, light green when young, maturing to a deep, rich green. In early spring, clusters of 2"–4"-wide bowl-shaped flowers of white, rose, pink, or maroon, often freckled or speckled at the center, top stems 12"–18" in height. After the petals drop, the calyx persists for several weeks, providing a considerable period of interest.

LIGHT CONDITIONS: Medium shade

SOIL/MOISTURE: Highly organic, well-drained soil, amended with compost or leaf mold

DESCRIPTION: Not as temperamental as their close relative the Christmas rose (*H. niger*), Lenten roses bloom a little later and bear several flowers per stem. Their clean, bold foliage serves as an attractive contrast for delicate ferns, astilbes, and goatsbeard in shaded or woodland settings. Try echoing the leaf shape with an underplanting of sweet woodruff. The flowers hold well in flower arrangements. Valuable as an underplanting for fine-leaved trees and shrubs, such as honey locust, mountain ash, Japanese maples, or *Neillia sinensis*.

Hosta 'Blue Angel'
(plantain lily, funkia)

Hosta 'Wogan Gold'
(plantain lily, funkia)

Iris versicolor
(blue iris, blue flag)

LEFT
Hosta plantaginea var.
grandiflora (August lily,
peace lily)

HOSTA 'BLUE ANGEL'

PRONUNCIATION: HOS-ta

COMMON NAME: Plantain lily, funkia

HOMELAND: Of garden origin

HARDINESS: USDA Zones 3–9

SIZE: 4' tall and wide

INTEREST: Huge, heavily puckered leaves of a beautiful blue-gray. Large clusters of white lilylike flowers open in mid- to late summer.

LIGHT CONDITIONS: Partial shade to shade

SOIL/MOISTURE: Well-drained but moisture-retentive, organic soil

DESCRIPTION: 'Blue Angel' is not one of the best choices for a ground-cover plant, for it increases slowly and takes its time to become established. Best grown as a magnificent specimen plant, perhaps to accent a rock outcropping or sculpture. Complement with great blue lobelia or willow-leaved gentian at waterside. 'Blue Angel' does well in containers as do many hostas; combine with blue wishbone flower (*Torenia fournieri*).

HOSTA PLANTAGINEA VAR. GRANDIFLORA

PRONUNCIATION: HOS-ta plan-tage-i-NEE-a var. grand-i-FLOR-a

COMMON NAME: August lily, peace lily

HOMELAND: China; variety of garden origin

HARDINESS: USDA Zones 3–9

SIZE: 24"–30" tall in bloom

INTEREST: Arching, heart-shaped leaves to 12" long. Intoxicatingly fragrant white 5" trumpets fill the evening air with perfume. Flowers mid- to late summer.

LIGHT CONDITIONS: Partial to dappled shade, or filtered light

SOIL/MOISTURE: Well-drained but moisture-retentive, organic soil

DESCRIPTION: Mass or combine with bold ferns such as royal fern or cinnamon fern, or partner with goatsbeard or Japanese anemones. An excellent and underused cut flower. Unless marred by slug damage, the leaves make attractive serving dishes for salads. Other cultivars such as 'Royal Standard' and 'Honey Bells' have the species in their parentage. 'Aphrodite' is a double form. All are wonderfully fragrant, and are exceptional specimens planted in an urn by the entrance to the shade garden.

HOSTA 'WOGAN GOLD'

PRONUNCIATION: HOS-ta

COMMON NAME: Plantain lily, funkia

HOMELAND: Of garden origin

HARDINESS: USDA Zones 3–9

SIZE: 6"–8"-tall mound of foliage; 8" across

INTEREST: Small, lance-shaped leaves of butter yellow are topped in late summer by spikes of small lavender flowers on 15" stems.

LIGHT CONDITIONS: Filtered or dappled shade is essential.

SOIL/MOISTURE: Well-drained but moisture-retentive, organic soil

DESCRIPTION: 'Wogan Gold' seems to make dark parts of the garden glow. Grow it in a container, set on a pedestal to punctuate the angle of a shaded path, or combine it with yellow monkey flowers. Carpet its feet with golden creeping Jennie, or complement it with *Corydalis lutea* or *Carex morrowii* 'Variegata'. Interesting planted under a *Cotoneaster* shrub as it is in Charles Cresson's Pennsylvania garden. As with all hostas, be alert for slug damage.

IRIS VERSICOLOR

PRONUNCIATION: EYE-ris VER-si-co-lor

COMMON NAME: Blue iris, blue flag

HOMELAND: Eastern Canada to Pennsylvania

HARDINESS: USDA Zones 3–8

SIZE: 2'–3' tall; 12"–15" across

INTEREST: In early to midsummer, fleeting blue to violet flowers, blotched with yellow and veined purple on the lower petals (falls), rise above a fan of broadly linear leaves.

LIGHT CONDITIONS: Light to dappled shade

SOIL/MOISTURE: Moist soil, of average fertility, that does not dry out. Wet meadows.

DESCRIPTION: Blue flags are attractive massed at water's edge, perhaps accented with an equal stand of yellow flags (*I. pseudacorus*) closeby, or as a companion for cattails or royal ferns. The succulent roots may be devastated by muskrats and other water wildlife. Take care in handling the rootstock, as it can cause dermatitis on sensitive skin. A glimpse of these plants blooming in the wild is a sight that will stay with you forever.

Marsilea mutica (water clover, pepperwort)

Pulmonaria saccharata 'Mrs. Moon' (lungwort, Bethlehem sage)

Polystichum polyblepharum (bristle fern, Japanese tassel fern)

RIGHT
Liriope muscari 'Variegata' (variegated lilyturf)

Liriope muscari 'Variegata'

PRONUNCIATION: leer-EE-o-pay mus-CAH-ree
COMMON NAME: Variegated blue lilyturf
HOMELAND: China, Japan; cultivar of garden origin
HARDINESS: USDA Zones 5–9
SIZE: 15"–24" tall; 12"–18" across

INTEREST: Evergreen strappy leaves, variegated with white and green stripes; the species has dark green foliage. Spikes of small purple flowers in late summer.
LIGHT CONDITIONS: Sun to shade
SOIL/MOISTURE: Well-drained, average soil

DESCRIPTION: Lilyturf is one of the most widely used plants for ground cover, especially in warm climates. The variegated sorts do not tolerate intense sun well, and prefer some shade, but variegated 'Silvery Sunproof', 12"–15" tall, is reputedly a sun-tolerant cultivar. Excellent massed with hostas, astilbes, epimediums, and ferns in low maintenance shaded areas. The variegated sorts are especially valuable in winter gardens, where their cream and green leaves enliven the dark days. 'Munroe's White', 12"–15" tall, has white flowers and solid green leaves; 'Big Blue', 8"–12" tall, has violet flowers. Mow to the ground in early spring to allow new growth to develop. Beware of slugs and snails.

Marsilea mutica

PRONUNCIATION: mar-SEE-lee-a MEW-tik-a
COMMON NAME: Water clover, pepperwort
HOMELAND: Australia
HARDINESS: USDA Zones 6–10
SIZE: Leaf stalks (stipes) to 3' long; leaflets floating
INTEREST: Two-toned glossy green, floating

leaflets, arranged like a 4-leaf clover, are accented with a central yellow blotch; about 2" across.
LIGHT CONDITIONS: Light shade
SOIL/MOISTURE: Grows in water, or alongside under boggy conditions.

DESCRIPTION: A true fern, water clover may be grown in bog gardens or beside ponds, where its attractive leaflets cover the surface of the water. It is also interesting in container water gardens in small spaces, to be admired up close. Other species sometimes offered for sale include the European water clover (*M. quadrifolia*) and the common nardoo (*M. drummondii*).

POLYSTICHUM POLYBLEPHARUM

PRONUNCIATION: pol-ee-STIK-um pol-ee-
BLEF-ar-um

COMMON NAME: Bristle fern, Japanese
tassel fern

HOMELAND: Japan and southern Korea

HARDINESS: USDA Zones 5–8

SIZE: 1'–2' tall; 2'–3' across

INTEREST: Arching habit, with evergreen, lustrous, dark fronds borne on scaly stems

LIGHT CONDITIONS: Partial shade

SOIL/MOISTURE: Rich, well-drained soil

DESCRIPTION: Bristle fern is one of a large genus of ferns suitable for temperate gardens. These are major players in foliage compositions for shaded places,
and they can be massed alone or interplanted with other shade-loving species.
Especially suitable for quiet sitting or meditation areas of the garden, perhaps
accompanied in spring with wood anemones, trilliums, dog's-tooth violets, and
primulas, and later with lilyturf or hostas.

PULMONARIA SACCHARATA 'MRS. MOON'

PRONUNCIATION: pul-mon-AIR-ee-a
sa-ka-RAH-ta

COMMON NAME: Bethlehem sage, lungwort

HOMELAND: Italy and France; cultivar of garden origin

HARDINESS: USDA Zones 3–8

SIZE: 12"–18" tall; up to 24" across

INTEREST: Small, trumpet-shaped flowers of

pink through purple, and then brilliant blue
open as the silver-dappled foliage emerges
and expands quickly to its ultimate 12" or
so in length. Flowers in early spring.

LIGHT CONDITIONS: Light, dappled, or filtered shade

SOIL/MOISTURE: Well-drained but moisture-
retentive soil

DESCRIPTION: Bethlehem sage makes a fine ground cover when massed as an
underplanting for shrubs or small trees. It is also effective as a woodland or
shade-border companion for sweet woodruff, epimediums, lilyturf, and other
superior shade lovers. The silver-spotted leaves shine in shady places. Many
new introductions such as 'Excaliber', 'Sissinghurst White', and 'Spilled Milk'
may be of hybrid origin. Most are prone to mildew if stressed by drought.

Rodgersia sambucifolia
(rodgersia)

Tovara virginiana
'Variegata'
[*Polygonum virginianum*]
(Virginia tovara)

Uvularia grandiflora
(great bells)

LEFT
Rodgersia pinnata
(featherleaf rodgersia)

RODGERSIA PINNATA

PRONUNCIATION: roe-JERZ-ee-a pi-NAH-ta

COMMON NAME: Featherleaf rodgersia

HOMELAND: China

HARDINESS: USDA Zones 5–8

SIZE: 3'–4' tall; up to 4' across

INTEREST: Bold, clean pinnate leaves, often bronzy when young, and sometimes turning brilliant copper color in fall. The dense, fuzzy inflorescence is composed of countless buff to rosy red flowers. A late-spring bloomer.

LIGHT CONDITIONS: Light or filtered shade

SOIL/MOISTURE: Rich, moist soil

DESCRIPTION: Grown as much for its striking foliage as for its flowers, featherleaf rodgersia is at its best beside water features such as ponds, streams, or lakes. Provide enough space for each plant to show off its potential. A good contrast for large ornamental grasses, but also attractive with moisture-loving irises and other bog plants. 'Superba' has darker pink flowers. *R. aesculifolia,* which has horse-chestnut-like leaves, is also reliable.

RODGERSIA SAMBUCIFOLIA

PRONUNCIATION: roe-JERZ-ee-a sam-BOOK-i-foe-lee-a

COMMON NAME: Rodgersia

HOMELAND: China and Japan

HARDINESS: USDA Zones 5–7

SIZE: 2'–6' tall; 4'–6' across, depending on species

INTEREST: Compound basal leaves often flushed with copper when young. The inflorescences are similar to those of astilbes; individual flowers lack petals but have rosy red or white sepals and stamens. Flowers early summer.

LIGHT CONDITIONS: Partial to light shade

SOIL/MOISTURE: Rich, moist soil, amended with compost or leaf mold

DESCRIPTION: Rodgersias are noble plants, grown especially for their bold leaves. *R. sambucifolia* is so named for its leaves, which, late in the season, resemble those of the elderberry. It is difficult to distinguish this plant from *R. pinnata,* but the leaf stem seems longer in the former. The horse-chestnut-like leaves of *R. aesculifolia* consist of usually 7 leaflets, each as long as 10". Large conical flower clusters of cream or pinkish red. Both are excellent beside water features, perhaps combined with the contrasting dissected foliage of ferns or astilbes or with the sword-shaped leaves of Japanese or Siberian iris.

Tovara virginiana 'Variegata'

PRONUNCIATION: toe-VAR-a vir-jin-ee-AY-na

COMMON NAME: Virginia tovara

HOMELAND: Eastern and central United States and eastern Canada; cultivar of garden origin

HARDINESS: USDA Zones 6–9

SIZE: 2'–3' tall; about 2' across

INTEREST: Attractive mounds of variegated foliage, splashed with ivory and cream. In the fall, spikes of cerise buds open greenish white. Flowers late summer to fall.

LIGHT CONDITIONS: Partial shade to shade, protected from wind

SOIL/MOISTURE: Moisture-retentive soil of average fertility

DESCRIPTION: 'Variegata' is striking in shade, especially in late summer and fall, when it assumes a prominent standing in the garden. It can be handsome underplanted with variegated pachysandra or gray-green native pachysandra. Although variegated goutweed might appear to be a bewitching companion, it is too aggressive to combine with tovara unless contained. 'Variegata' has frequently masqueraded in the trade for the more popular cultivar 'Painter's Palette', which is identified by a chocolate chevron on each leaf.

Uvularia grandiflora

PRONUNCIATION: ewe-vew-LAY-ree-a grand-i-FLOR-a

COMMON NAME: Great bells

HOMELAND: Quebec to North Dakota, and Georgia to Oklahoma

HARDINESS: USDA Zones 3–9

SIZE: 12"–24" tall; 18" across

INTEREST: Clasping, light green, oblong leaves. Solitary and terminal, the lemon yellow, nodding, lilylike flowers bloom in spring.

LIGHT CONDITIONS: Partial shade to shade

SOIL/MOISTURE: Moist, acidic soil

DESCRIPTION: Big merrybells is a lovely native woodlander and mixes well with other woodland species. Plant it with bleeding hearts, primroses, creeping phlox, and false Solomon's seal for an interesting spring picture. When the heat of summer commences, big merrybells dies back and becomes summer-dormant. Self-seeds readily. Look for other members of this genus of wonderful woodlanders.

Ground
Covers and
Vines

Ground Covers and Vines

A familiarity with the hierarchy of the forest helps shade garden design. On top of the tree canopy, vines clambor in search of light; down below are fallen leaves, herbaceous ephemerals, and ground covers. In nature, ground covers trap leaf-litter to replenish soil, fight erosion, and prevent weeds from getting a foothold. For us, they also present a tidy appearance and unify plantings. Discussing vines and ground covers might seem odd, except that quite a few are both. In deep shade, English ivy will clothe the ground; but when the running stems meet a vertical obstacle, up it goes. (Ivy and many other vines should not be planted in proximity to natural areas as they can become pests.)

Ivy, *Vinca minor*, and *Pachysandra terminalis* are the workhorse ground covers, though not necessarily the prettiest. *Pachysandra*, or Japanese spurge, has plasticlike, army green leaves;

however, its beautiful cousin is the native Allegheny spurge (*P. procumbens*), whose leaves are matte green in summer, green with silver in winter, and bronze when new. Other aliens have native cousins. The wild gingers include native *Asarum canadensis*, mottled *A. shuttleworthii*, arrowhead *A. arrifolium*, and their counterparts including evergreen *A. europeum*.

The wild gingers have refined foliage, but there are ground covers with showier leaves and flowers such as *Lamium maculatum* 'White Nancy' with silvery leaves and white flowers, and *Pulmonaria* cultivars with platinum splashes on their leaves, and blue flowers. *Epimedium*, or barrenworts, are tiny to midsized plants for dry shade with white, violet, orange, yellow, purple, red, or bicolor blossoms.

Asarum and *Epimedium* are good to cover vine roots that like it cool. If there is sunshine above your garden, then you will be able to choose from nearly any vine. Most of us have some version of that condition, perhaps a half day of sunshine on pergolas, trellises, arbors, high fences, walls, and in some cases, trees. Flowering bowers include natives *Lonicera sempervirens* and *Campsis radicans*. Climbing hydrangea (*Hydrangea petiolaris*) has white flowers and will eventually cover a wall with glossy green leaves. Have patience; vines sleep, creep, and then leap!

Asarum shuttleworthii (wild ginger)

Bergenia cordifolia (heartleaf bergenia)

Chrysogonum virginianum (green 'n gold)

RIGHT
Ajuga reptans 'Burgundy Glow' (bugleweed)

AJUGA REPTANS 'BURGUNDY GLOW'

PRONUNCIATION: a-JEW-gah REP-tanz

COMMON NAME: Bugleweed

HOMELAND: Europe; cultivar of garden origin

HARDINESS: USDA Zones 3–9

SIZE: 4″–12″ tall; to 2′ across

INTEREST: Tight rosettes of semievergreen foliage, gray-green splashed with cream and burgundy. Tiny purplish blue flowers line 4″ spikes in mid- to late spring.

LIGHT CONDITIONS: Partial to light shade

SOIL/MOISTURE: Average well-drained soil is best, but is tolerant of damp soils unless they are compacted.

DESCRIPTION: This striking foliage plant is less aggressive than other cultivars of *A. reptans* or the species. It is suitable in shaded rock gardens, between paving stones, and alongside pathways, even at the front of flower borders. Try it at the feet of *Berberis thunbergii* 'Atropurpurea' or 'Crimson Pygmy', or interplant with *Heuchera* 'Palace Purple' or one of the new cultivars such as 'Ruby Veil'.

ASARUM SHUTTLEWORTHII

PRONUNCIATION: a-SAR-um shut-tul-WERTH-ee-eye

COMMON NAME: Wild ginger

HOMELAND: North temperate regions

HARDINESS: USDA Zones 6–8

SIZE: 6″–12″ tall and 8″–12″ across, depending on species

INTEREST: Heart-shaped, glossy, evergreen leaves, sometimes variegated, or matte green, deciduous foliage. Flowers spring.

LIGHT CONDITIONS: Medium to heavy shade

SOIL/MOISTURE: Slightly acid, moisture-retentive soil, amended with organic matter

DESCRIPTION: This is one of several evergreen species, of which the most widely grown is European wild ginger (*A. europaeum*), which does best in cool climates and combines well with ferns and hostas. The natives such as *A. shuttleworthii* and *A. hartwegii*, both of which have exquisite mottled leaves, are splendid in warmer climes. Deciduous *A. canadense* with large matte green leaves is most suitable in woodland plantings with other natives and is also good in the South.

BERGENIA CORDIFOLIA

PRONUNCIATION: ber-GEN-i-a
kor-di-FOE-lee-a

COMMON NAME: Heartleaf bergenia

HOMELAND: Siberia

HARDINESS: USDA Zones 3—8

SIZE: 12"—18" tall and as wide

INTEREST: Basal rosettes of glossy, cabbage-shaped foliage, evergreen in all but the most severe climates. Many cultivars have attractive bronze or liver color leaves in cold weather. Flowers spring and sporadically.

LIGHT CONDITIONS: Partial shade, especially during the heat of the day

SOIL/MOISTURE: Damp but not wet soil, of average fertility

DESCRIPTION: The medium-sized but substantial leaves of bergenia show off best in bold plantings with astilbes or ferns as a foil. Especially effective near water features. Popular cultivars include white-flowered 'Bressingham White' and 'Perfecta' with rosy red flowers.

CHRYSOGONUM VIRGINIANUM

PRONUNCIATION: kris-OG-o-num vir-jin-ee-AYE-num

COMMON NAME: Green 'n gold

HOMELAND: Native; Pennsylvania and West Virginia to Florida and Louisiana

HARDINESS: USDA Zones 5—9

SIZE: 6"—9" tall; 9"—12" across

INTEREST: Bright yellow, 1" daisylike flowers are borne over neat rosettes of softly hairy, fresh green leaves in spring, and sporadically through the season, except in intense heat.

LIGHT CONDITIONS: Light to dappled shade in the North; deeper shade in hot zones

SOIL/MOISTURE: Moist, well-drained soil, amended with compost or leaf mold

DESCRIPTION: Excellent in native plant gardens and light woodlands. Useful as a ground cover under rhododendrons, azaleas, and mountain laurels, as well as other shrubs. Makes a striking springtime carpet under white birches. Growers are interested in this intermittantly blooming, shade-tolerant ground cover, and are introducing cultivars such as 'Allen Bush' and 'Mark Viette'.

Convallaria majalis
(lily-of-the-valley)

Galium odoratum
(sweet woodruff)

Lamium maculatum
'White Nancy'
(spotted dead nettle)

LEFT
Hedera helix 'Pedata'
(bird's-foot ivy)

CONVALLARIA MAJALIS

PRONUNCIATION: kon-val-AIR-ee-a maj-A-lis
COMMON NAME: Lily-of-the-valley
HOMELAND: North temperate regions
HARDINESS: USDA Zones 2–7
SIZE: 10″–12″ tall; spreading 2′–3′ wide
INTEREST: Bright green basal leaves that remain in good condition until late summer

unless stressed unduly by drought. In spring, drooping spikes of dangling, pure white, very fragrant flowers open.

LIGHT CONDITIONS: Medium to partial shade
SOIL/MOISTURE: Moist, organic soil, amended with leaf mold or compost

DESCRIPTION: Lily-of-the-valley has the fragrance that carries one back to one's childhood and Grandma's garden. It is a staple of shaded cottage gardens but needs space to roam. Excellent as a ground cover in light woodland areas, where it mixes well with bloodroot and sweet woodruff for a foliage combination. Cut it back when the leaves become shabby. The roots (pips) can be lifted and forced into flower indoors. 'Fortin's Giant' is a little taller than the species, with larger flowers; 'Rosea' has dirty pink flowers; and 'Aureovariegata' ['Striata', 'Variegata'] has yellow stripes on the leaves. Why spoil perfection?

GALIUM ODORATUM

PRONUNCIATION: gay-LEEE-um o-dor-AH-tum
COMMON NAME: Sweet woodruff
HOMELAND: Europe
HARDINESS: USDA Zones 4–8
SIZE: 6″–9″ tall; to 12″–15″ across
INTEREST: Whorls of fresh green, pointed leaves are accented with clusters of tiny

white flowers in spring. Tan winter foliage.

LIGHT CONDITIONS: Light to partial shade in the North; deeper shade in hot zones
SOIL/MOISTURE: Well-drained but moisture-retentive soil, although is tolerant of drier conditions in cool areas.

DESCRIPTION: This delicate-looking low-growing herb, fragrant of newly mown hay and used to flavor May wine, makes an excellent ground cover in filtered shade beneath trees and shrubs. It combines well with epimediums, lungworts (*Pulmonaria* spp.), hellebores, and Solomon's seal (*Polygonatum* spp.) in shaded informal flower gardens. Cut back in early spring to allow for new growth. Can become invasive.

HEDERA HELIX 'PEDATA'

PRONUNCIATION: HED-er-a HEE-liks

COMMON NAME: Bird's-foot ivy

HOMELAND: Caucasus mountains; cultivar of garden origin

HARDINESS: USDA Zones 4–9

SIZE: 6"–8" tall as a ground cover, but may climb to 50' or more

INTEREST: Fine-textured, dark green, evergreen foliage shaped like a bird's foot

LIGHT CONDITIONS: Light to deep shade; protect from strong winter sun.

SOIL/MOISTURE: Average to damp, well-drained soil with plenty of organic matter is best, but tolerates drier conditions.

DESCRIPTION: A refined ground-cover plant. Underplant with spring-flowering small daffodils and narcissus, and with *Colchicum* for a fall display. Highlight with *Liriope muscari* 'Variegata' or variegated hostas such as 'Antioch' or *Hosta undulata* var. *erromena;* or allow *Vinca major* 'Variegata' to trail across it to lighten the scene.

LAMIUM MACULATUM 'WHITE NANCY'

PRONUNCIATION: LAY-mee-um mak-yew-LAH-tum

COMMON NAME: Spotted dead nettle

HOMELAND: Europe and western Asia; cultivar of garden origin

HARDINESS: USDA Zones 3–8

SIZE: 8"–10" tall; spreading 10"–12" across

INTEREST: Evergreen silver leaves frosted with emerald. Spikes of white flowers in spring.

LIGHT CONDITIONS: Filtered light

SOIL/MOISTURE: Average well-drained soil, amended with compost or leaf mold.

DESCRIPTION: Other cultivars of *L. maculatum* include 'Beacon Silver', a similar but slightly taller plant with purplish flowers, which is larger and more aggressive than 'White Nancy'. 'Shell Pink' has pale pink flowers. 'Beedham's White' has bright yellow and white foliage and white flowers; it demands good shade cover to avoid sunburn. 'Chequers' has purplish flowers, and green leaves flashed down the center with silver; it is perhaps at its most striking during very cold weather when the undersides of the leaves become purplish and the silver flash stands out. It tends toward being invasive. All these make superior ground-cover plants. In the photo, 'White Nancy' is paired with *Parochetus communis,* a subtropical creeping herb.

Pachysandra procumbens
(Allegheny spurge)

Symphytum grandiflorum
(large-flowered comfrey)

Vinca minor (vinca,
periwinkle, myrtle)

RIGHT
Phlox stolonifera
(creeping phlox)

PACHYSANDRA PROCUMBENS

PRONUNCIATION: **pak-i-SAN-dra pro-KUM-benz**
COMMON NAME: **Allegheny spurge**
HOMELAND: **Native; eastern Kentucky, West Virginia to Florida and Louisiana**
HARDINESS: **USDA Zones 4–9**
SIZE: **6″–12″ tall and wide**
INTEREST: **Attractive matte gray-green leaves, often mottled with brown, which regrettably turn to green later in the season. Sends up spikes of whitish or pink flowers in spring.**
LIGHT CONDITIONS: **Partial to full shade**
SOIL/MOISTURE: **Moist, organic soil on the acid side**

DESCRIPTION: This less commonly used ground-cover plant is evergreen in all but the coldest climates. It deserves a wider audience and is especially suitable for underplanting native azaleas in natural woodland settings. New growth is coppery green. Summer leaves are matte green. Winter color is celadon-silver over deep green. Propagate by division in early spring. Grab a stem and pull hard and fast. It will break off and have one or two roots attached. Plant this at once.

PHLOX STOLONIFERA

PRONUNCIATION: **FLOX sto-lon-IF-e-ra**
COMMON NAME: **Creeping phlox**
HOMELAND: **Native; Pennsylvania to Georgia**
HARDINESS: **USDA Zones 2–8**
SIZE: **6″–12″ tall; about 12″ wide**
INTEREST: **Low-growing mats of evergreen foliage are covered in spring with 12″-tall flowering stems crowned with clusters of bright pink flowers.**
LIGHT CONDITIONS: **Partial shade to shade**
SOIL/MOISTURE: **Moist woodland-type soil, amended with plenty of compost or leaf mold**

DESCRIPTION: Several of the cultivars are superior to the species: 'Bruce's White' has large, clean white flowers with a yellow eye; 'Blue Ridge' has lavender-blue flowers; 'Pink Ridge' is a mauve pink. An ideal plant to clothe an edge-of-woodland floor, creeping phlox may also be used in the rock garden or as a ground cover in informal parts of the garden. Underplant with crocus and miniature daffodils for spring and with *Colchicum* and autumn crocus for fall interest.

SYMPHYTUM GRANDIFLORUM

PRONUNCIATION: sim-FIE-tum grand-i-FLOR-um

COMMON NAME: Large-flowered comfrey

HOMELAND: Caucasus region

HARDINESS: USDA Zones 3–8

SIZE: 12″–15″ tall; 15″–18″ across

INTEREST: Coarsely hairy stems and leaves form a dense mat, which is accented in spring and sporadically later with pale yellow, tubular bells.

LIGHT CONDITIONS: Partial shade

SOIL/MOISTURE: Tolerant of dry conditions, but is at its best in moist but well-drained, organic soil.

DESCRIPTION: Several cultivars have come into the trade recently. 'Blue Glocken' has pale blue flower stems under 10″ tall. 'Variegata' has attractive cream-variegated foliage. The British selections 'Hidcote Blue' and 'Hidcote Pink', sometimes listed as *S. ibericum* or *S. caucasicum,* have, respectively, blue and white or pink and white flowers. One of the most reliable plants to mass as a shade ground cover.

VINCA MINOR

PRONUNCIATION: VING-ka MINE-or

COMMON NAME: Vinca, periwinkle, myrtle

HOMELAND: Europe

HARDINESS: USDA Zones 4–9

SIZE: 6″–12″ tall; widely spreading

INTEREST: Slightly glossy, evergreen leaves on creeping stems. Bears clear blue 1½″ pinwheel flowers in spring.

LIGHT CONDITIONS: Light to deep shade

SOIL/MOISTURE: Moist, well-drained soil that is not compacted

DESCRIPTION: One of the best plants for deep shade, but in that circumstance, flowering is sparse. Plant closely for best effect. Superior cultivars include 'Sterling Silver', which has white-edged leaves, and 'Atropurpurea', which is compact and has dusky purple flowers. Clump-forming 'Miss Jekyll' is white flowered. Underplant with bulbs for spring or fall, or pair with taller ferns, hostas, or astilbes. Do not let this plant get away—especially into wild areas.

Campsis radicans
(trumpet vine)

Clematis armandii (armand
or evergreen clematis)

Hedera helix
(English ivy)

LEFT
Ampelopsis brevipedunculata
'Elegans' (variegated
porcelain berry)

AMPELOPSIS BREVIPEDUNCULATA 'ELEGANS'

PRONUNCIATION: am-pel-OP-sis brev-i-ped-unk-u-LAY-ta

COMMON NAME: Variegated porcelain berry

HOMELAND: China, Korea, and Japan; cultivar of garden origin

HARDINESS: USDA Zones 4–8

SIZE: 3'–10' vining

INTEREST: Grapelike leaves variegated in white and tinged with pink when young; new growth has magenta stems. Pink, then purple and speckled deep turquoise, pea-sized berries. Flowers early summer.

LIGHT CONDITIONS: Partial shade

SOIL/MOISTURE: Well-drained soil, amended with organic matter

DESCRIPTION: This tendril climber makes an attractive light screen. Not as rampant as the species, 'Elegans' is better suited to smaller gardens, where its white-splashed leaves enliven dark spots. The intense color of the berries is somewhat startling and adds fall interest. Provide a trellis or screen for support, or allow it to drape itself over conveniently close shrubs. Partner with *Clematis recta* for spring bloom and *C. terniflora* for the fall. Avoid the all-green species, which quickly becomes a serious pest.

CAMPSIS RADICANS

PRONUNCIATION: KAMP-sis RAD-i-kanz

COMMON NAME: Trumpet vine

HOMELAND: Native; Pennsylvania to Missouri, Florida, and Texas

HARDINESS: USDA Zones 4–9

SIZE: 30' or more climber; 3'–5' wide

INTEREST: Clusters of 2"-long trumpet flowers of bright orange-red from midsummer to early fall

LIGHT CONDITIONS: Full sun to light shade

SOIL/MOISTURE: Tolerant of most soils; overly rich soil promotes rampant growth.

DESCRIPTION: This showy native vine is excellent for clothing trellises, arbors, and other sturdy structures rapidly. It can also be used to form a dense screen where privacy is required. The flowers, which vary in color, are most attractive to hummingbirds. The yellow form 'Flava' is preferred by some people, but not by hummingbirds; grow one of each intertwined. Spur-prune hard in spring. Look out for ground suckers. Do not plant near wild areas.

CLEMATIS ARMANDII

PRONUNCIATION: **KLEM-a-tis ar-MAN-dee-eye**

COMMON NAME: **Armand or evergreen clematis**

HOMELAND: **Central and western China**

HARDINESS: **USDA Zones 7–10**

SIZE: **20' or more climbing; as wide or more**

INTEREST: **Deep green, leathery, pointed leaves are covered with hundreds of clusters of frothy white, fragrant flowers in spring.**

LIGHT CONDITIONS: **Partial shade**

SOIL/MOISTURE: **Moist, highly organic soil that provides a cool root run**

DESCRIPTION: Grown especially for its fine foliage, *Clematis armandii* should be pruned immediately after flowering to allow for new growth. This rampant vine may need to be contained when it is growing well. Allow it to scramble over the top of a wall or to drape itself through a tree or large shrub. 'Snowdrift' has pure white flowers; white 'Apple Blossom' shows blush pink on the reverse.

HEDERA HELIX

PRONUNCIATION: **HED-er-a HEE-liks**

COMMON NAME: **English ivy**

HOMELAND: **Caucasus mountains**

HARDINESS: **USDA Zones 4–9**

SIZE: **70'–90' or more**

INTEREST: **Evergreen, lobed leaves, often accented with white or yellowish veins. The adult foliage, which is not lobed, flowers, and black berries appear only on mature plants.**

LIGHT CONDITIONS: **Partial shade to shade; protect from winter sun.**

SOIL/MOISTURE: **Tolerates acid and alkaline soil; organic soil that is well drained and moist is ideal.**

DESCRIPTION: There are countless forms, selections, and cultivars of this popular vine, which may also be used as a ground cover. Some of the best include hardy forms: '238th Street', superior because it does not succumb to winter burn; 'Baltica', which has smaller than normal leaves; and 'Bulgaria', which is possibly the hardiest of all. 'Glacier' is a popular cultivar with gray-green leaves variegated with white. 'Buttercup' has clear yellow leaves, especially when they are young. The green leaves of 'Goldheart' have a yellow blotch in the center of each. Effective climbing on trees and buildings. Prune to keep within bounds.

Hydrangea petiolaris
(climbing hydrangea)

Parthenocissus tricuspidata
(Boston ivy)

Schisandra chinensis
(magnolia vine)

Right
Lonicera ✕ *heckrottii*
(everblooming or
goldflame honeysuckle)

HYDRANGEA PETIOLARIS [H. anomala spp. petiolaris]

PRONUNCIATION: hi-DRAN-jee-a pet-ee-o-LAR-is

COMMON NAME: Climbing hydrangea

HOMELAND: Japan and China

HARDINESS: USDA Zones 4–8

SIZE: 60'–90' or more; 3'–5' wide

INTEREST: Lustrous dark green foliage held in horizontal planes. In midsummer the branches are adorned with terminal flat-topped clusters of showy, white, sterile flowers surrounding tiny, fertile inner flowers. Cinnamon-colored exfoliating bark with age.

LIGHT CONDITIONS: Full sun to shade

SOIL/MOISTURE: Well-drained but moist soil, enriched with organic matter

DESCRIPTION: Slow to become established, this vine ultimately will cover fences, trees, buildings, and other structures with amazing speed, attaching itself by small rootlets. It is interesting at all seasons and is certainly among the very best vines. Best to start in a container to avoid excessive root disturbance at planting time. Grow with look-alike *Schizophragma hydrangeoides* to extend flower show.

LONICERA × HECKROTTII

PRONUNCIATION: lon-ISS-er-a × hek-ROT-ee-eye

COMMON NAME: Everblooming or goldflame honeysuckle

HOMELAND: Of garden origin

HARDINESS: USDA Zones 4–9

SIZE: 10'–20' tall; 2' wide

INTEREST: Carmine red flower buds open to reveal butter yellow insides with a light fragrance. Pink stems and semievergreen, blue-green foliage. Flowers late spring and sporadically.

LIGHT CONDITIONS: Light, partial, to dappled shade

SOIL/MOISTURE: Soil of rich to average fertility that does not dry out excessively

DESCRIPTION: One of the best climbers of the genus, goldflame honeysuckle blooms from late spring right through until fall. Furnish it with an arch, trellis, or pergola on which to climb and show off its beautiful foliage and flowers, preferably close to a sitting area where the fragrance can be appreciated. Can be grown as a mounded shrub if pruned routinely. Prone to mildew if stressed, and aphids if growth is too juicy from nitrogen fertilizer; dislodge the insects with a blast from the garden hose. Attractive to hummingbirds.

PARTHENOCISSUS TRICUSPIDATA

PRONUNCIATION: par-the-no-CIS-us tri-kus-pi-DA-ta

COMMON NAME: Boston ivy

HOMELAND: Japan and central China

HARDINESS: USDA Zones 4–8

SIZE: Up to 90' or more; 5'–10' wide

INTEREST: Deciduous 3-lobed leaves, to 8" across and shaped like a duck's foot, turn yellow, red, to bronzy black in fall. Semievergreen in mild climates. Flowers insignificant.

LIGHT CONDITIONS: Full sun to partial shade

SOIL/MOISTURE: Tolerant of a wide range of soils, and even dry conditions once established

DESCRIPTION: One of the most popular climbing plants for covering buildings, pillars, and other stonework, especially under urban conditions, where it tolerates pollution well. This is the ivy of the "Ivy League." 'Lowii' has small frilly leaves; 'Veitchii' also has small leaves, which are purplish when young. 'Fenway' is a new gold-leafed cultivar found growing on the wall of the famed Boston ballpark.

SCHISANDRA CHINENSIS

PRONUNCIATION: sky-SAN-dra chi-NEN-sis

COMMON NAME: Magnolia vine

HOMELAND: Eastern Asia

HARDINESS: USDA Zones 6–9

SIZE: Up to 25'; 3'–5' wide

INTEREST: This woody deciduous vine has lustrous, toothed leaves to 4" long and, in early summer, clusters of small, fragrant, creamy white flowers. These are followed in fall by striking pendent clusters of scarlet fruits.

LIGHT CONDITIONS: Partial shade

SOIL/MOISTURE: Well-drained, fertile soil that remains moist

DESCRIPTION: This twiner needs support on which to grow, or it can be allowed to scramble over rocks, walls, or tree stumps. Prune in late winter to contain excessive growth. Attractive when planted with yews (*Taxus* spp.) or other dark evergreens, so that the berries are displayed to good advantage in fall. I've even seen this vine bloom inside of yews, in deep shade.

Appendix

The Best Hostas

Once you begin to grow hostas, America's favorite perennial, you will start to make friends—plants and people. You
may even decide to join the American Hosta Society (AHS)
to receive their publications and attend local, regional, or
national meetings, where you might come across the latest
introduction and perhaps obtain a division of an unusual
variety to add to your collection.

Every year the AHS conducts a popularity poll among its
members for favorite hostas. These people do not just nom-
inate a pretty face. Plants are sturdy, vigorous, dependable,
slug-resistent, and unusual. The following list has some top
choices from the last few years.

Hosta 'Antioch'—medium ground cover; silver blue

H. 'August Moon'—medium; spade-shaped, pale gold, keeps color

H. fluctuans 'Variegata'—large; green stems, irregular brilliant yellow edges

H. 'Francee'—ground cover; deep green with white

H. 'Frances Williams'—large; blue-edged with primrose yellow; a best-seller

H. 'Gold Standard'—large; green-edged gold

H. 'Golden Tiara'—like a small version of 'Gold Standard'

H. 'Great Expectations'—blue-green, light yellow center

H. 'Halcyon'—medium; aristocratic, variegated upright, cream in spring

H. 'Kabitan'—ground cover; sickle-shaped, brilliant yellow green streaks

H. 'Krossa Regal'—medium; upright, vase shape; one of my favorites

H. 'Love Pat'—medium; blue, puckered cups

H. montana 'Aureomarginata'—variegated, vase shape when emerging

H. 'Piedmont Gold'—large; twist to leaves

H. sieboldiana 'Elegans'—large; huge puckered blue-green; all-time great

H. 'Sum and Substance'—huge; gold plant; most popular with AHS

H. 'Sun Power'—large; twisted leaves, rapid grower, nonfading gold

H. tokudama 'Aureonebulosa'—medium; blue, green margins, yellow center

H. ventricosa 'Aureo-marginata'—ground cover; yellow margin turns white

For AHS membership information, write to:

American Hosta Society
Robyn Duback
7802 NE 63rd Street
Vancouver, WA 98662

Hosta Sources

Andre Viette Farm & Nursery
Route 1, Box 16
State Route 608
Fishersville, VA 22939
(703) 943-2315
*Huge list including many perennials
classified for shade. Catalog: $2*

Crownsville Nursery
P.O. Box 797
Crownsville, MD 21032
(301) 923-2212
*Outstanding list with good descrip-
tions; hosta and familiar and
unusual perennials. Catalog: $2*

Fairway Enterprises
114 The Fairway
Alber Lea, MN 56007
(507) 373-5290
List: SASE

Meadowlake Gardens
Route 4,. Box 709
Walterboro, SC 29488
(803) 844-2359 or 844-2545
Catalog: $2

Piedmont Gardens
533-577 Piedmont Street
Waterbury, CT 06706
(203) 754-8534 or 754-3535
Catalog: $.50

Plant Delights Nursery, Inc.
9241 Sauls Road
Raleigh, NC 27603
(919) 772-4794
*Conifers, flowering shrubs, herbaceous
perennials, grasses, hostas.
Catalog: $2*

Walden-West
5744 Crooked Finger Road
NE
Scotts Mills, OR 97375
(503) 873-6875
Catalog: free

The Best Ferns

Besides hostas, ferns might be the most useful—and certainly most diverse—foliage plants. This is not one genus (as *Hosta* is), but a huge group of nonflowering plants—typified by feathery fronds—divided (pinnate) with leaflets on either sides of the stem; or bipinnate, when the pinnate leaves are dissected again. Below is a list of some of my favorite easy-to-grow species. Plant them among rocks or in colonies to look as natural as possible. But watch out: It is easy to get hooked on ferns. You might even want to join the American Fern Society or a regional-specific group.

Adiantum aleuticum, western
maidenhair

A. pedatum, northern maidenhair

Athyrium angustum, northern lady
fern

A. felix-femina, European lady
fern

A. nipponicum 'Pictum,' Japanese
painted fern

A. thelypteroides, silvery glade fern

Blechnum spicant, deer fern

Crytomium fortunei, crytomium

Cystopteris bulbifera, bladder fern

C. fragilis, fragile fern

Dennstaedtia punctilobula, hay-
scented fern

Diplazium pycnocarpon, narrow-
leafed pleenwort, glade fern

Dryopteris spp. (Most species of
the wood or shelid ferns are
easy to grow)

D. erythrosora, autumn fern

D. felix-mas, male fern

D. goldiana, Goldie's fern

*Matteuccia pensylvanica (M.
struthiopteris),* ostrich fern

Onoclea sensibilis, sensitive fern

Osmunda cinnamomea, cinnamon
fern

O. claytonia, interrupted fern

O. regalis, royal fern

Polystichum acrostichoides,
Christmas fern (evergreen
and very easy)

P. braunii, Braun's holly fern

P. makinoi, Makino's holly fern

P. munitum, Western sword fern

Thelypteris noveboracensis, New
York fern

T. phegopteris, narrow beech fern

Woodwardia areolata, netted chain
fern

**For information about mem-
bership in the national organi-
zation write to:**

American Fern Society
Dr. Richard L. Hauke
456 McGill Place
Atlanta, GA 30312

FERN SOURCES

Eco-Gardens
P.O. Box 1227
Decatur, GA 30031
(404) 294-6468
*Native Eastern wildflowers, trees,
    shrubs, ferns, and exotics.
    Catalog: $2*

Fancy Fronds
1911 Fourth Avenue West
Seattle, WA 98119
*Ferns from everywhere, excellent
    source. Catalog: $1*

Foliage Gardens
2003 128th Avenue SE
Bellevue, WA 98005
(206) 747-2998
Ferns: all spore-grown. Catalog: $1

Forestfarm
990 Tetherow Road
Williams, OR 97544
(503) 846-6963
*Excellent source of woody natives and
    unusual plants. Informative cata-
    log; one of the best sources.
    Catalog: $3*

Roslyn Nursery
211 Burrs Lane
Dix Hills, NY 11746
(516) 643-9347

*Extensive catalog of rare and familiar
    woody plants, rhododendrons,
    pieris, kalmias, azaleas.
    Catalog: $2*

Russell Graham
4030 Eagle Crest Road NW
Salem, OR 97304
(503) 362-1135
*Wonderful collection of ferns, shade
    plants, and bulbs. Catalog: $2*

Siskiyou Rare Plant Nursery
2825 Cummings Road
Medford, OR 97501
(503) 772-6846
*Incredible selection of wild plants: spe-
    cializing in, but not limited to,
    alpines and rock-garden plants.
    Catalog: $2*

We-Du Nurseries
Route 5, Box 724
Marion, NC 28752
(704) 738-8300
Woodland plants. Catalog: $1

Wild Earth Native Plant
    Nursery
49 Mead Avenue
Freehold, NJ
(908) 780-5661
A new nursery worth trying.

Mail-Order
Nurseries

Ambergate Gardens
8015 Krey Avenue
Waconia, MN 55387
(612) 443-2248
*Hostas, unusual perennials, Martagon
    lilies. Catalog: $2*

Andre Viette Farm & Nursery
Route 1, Box 16
State Route 608
Fishersville, VA 22939
(703) 943-2315
*Huge list including many perennials
    classified for shade. Catalog: $2*

The Bovees Nursery
1737 Southwest Coronado
Portland, OR 97219
(503) 244-9341
*Flowering shrubs, trees, perennials,
    vines, tropical rhododendrons.
    Catalog: $2*

Briarwood Gardens
14 Gully Lane
East Sandwich, MA 02537
(508) 888-2146
Rhododendrons. Catalog: $1

Brown's Kalmia and Azalea
    Nursery
8527 Semiahmoo Drive
Blaine, WA 98230
(206) 371-2489
*Kalmia, azaleas.
    List: $1*

Camellia Forest Nursery
P.O. Box 291
125 Carolina Forest
Chapel Hill, NC 27516
(919) 967-5529
*Camellias, conifers.
    Catalog: $1*

Caprice Nursery
15425 Southwest Pleasant Hill
    Road
Sherwood, OR 97140
(503) 625-7241
Peonies, Japanese and Siberian irises,
    hemerocallis, hostas. Catalog: $2

Carlson's Gardens
P.O. Box 305 NSG
South Salem, NY 10590
(914) 763-5958
Native azaleas; nothern grown and
    acclimated. Catalog: $2

Carroll Gardens
P.O. Box 310
444 East Main Street
Westminster, MD 21157
(800) 638-6334
Extensive, well-written catalog.
    Catalog: $2

Crownsville Nursery
P.O. Box 797
Crownsville, MD 21032
(301) 923-2212
Outstanding list with good descrip-
    tions; hostas and familiar and
    unusual perennials. Catalog: $2

The Cummins Gardens
22 Robertsville Road
Marlboro, NJ 07746
(201) 536-2591

Dwarf and unusual rhododendrons
    and azaleas, mountain laurels.
    Catalog: $2

Eastern Plant Specialties
P.O. Box 226
Georgetown, ME 04548
(207) 371-2888
Dwarf conifers, flowering shrubs,
    trees, rhododendrons, kalmia,
    azaleas. Catalog: $2

Eco-Gardens
P.O. Box 1227
Decatur, GA 30031
(404) 294-6468
Native Eastern wildflowers, trees,
    shrubs, ferns, and exotics.
    Catalog: $2

Forestfarm
990 Tetherow Road
Williams, OR 97544
(503) 846-6963
Excellent source of woody natives and
    unusual plants. Informative cata-
    log: one of the best sources.
    Catalog: $3

Gilson Gardens
P.O. Box 277
U.S. Route 20
Perry, OH 44081
(216) 259-4845
Perennials and ground covers.
    Catalog: free

Gossler Farms Nursery
1200 Weaver Road
Springfield, OR 97478-9663
(503) 746-3922 or 747-0749
*Magnolias and stewartia; 200–300
varieties of plants. Catalog: $1*

Greer Gardens
1280 Goodpasture Island Road
Eugene, OR 97401-1794
(503) 686-8266
*Excellent source of rhododendrons;
extensive list. Japanese maples and
rare shrubs. Catalog: $3*

Hall Rhododendrons
P.O. Box 62
6924 Highway 38
Drain, OR 97435
(503) 836-2290
*Over 1,600 varieties of rhododen-
dron. Catalog: $1*

Heronswood Nursery, Ltd.
7530 288th Street NE
Kingston, WA 98346
(206) 297-4172
*Conifers, flowering shrubs, trees,
herbaceous plants. Catalog: $3*

Holly Haven Hybrids
136 Sandwood Road
Knoxville, TN 37923-5564
Hollies. List: long SASE

Ivies of the World
P.O. Box 408
Highway 42
Weirsdale, FL 32195
(904) 821-2201 or 2322
*Over 200 varieties of ivies—hardy
and tender. Catalog: $1.50*

Jernigan Gardens
Route 6, Box 593
Dunn, NC 28334
(919) 567-2135
Ferns, daylilies, irises. List: SASE

Kelleygreen Rhododendron
    Nursery
6924 Highway 38
Drain, OR 97435
(503) 836-2290
*Rhododendron, azaleas, pieris, kalmias,
and Japanese maples. Catalog: $1.25*

Kelly's Plant World
10266 East Princeton
Sanger, CA 93657
(209) 294-7676 or 292-3505
*Ligularia, tricyrtis, summer-blooming
bulbs. Catalog: free*

Klehm Nursery
4210 North Duncan Road
Champagne, IL 61821
(800) 553-3715
*Herbaceous perennials, ferns, Siberian
iris, Hemerocallis, hostas,
peonies. Catalog: $4*

Lamb Nurseries
East 101 Sharp Avenue
Spokane, WA 99202
(509) 328-7956
Perennials for shade. Catalog: free

Lamtree Farm
2323 Copeland Road
Warrensville, NC 28693
(910) 385-6144
Native propagated trees and shrubs:
    Franklinia, Steartia, Styrax,
    Halesia, Rhododendron,
    Azalea, Kalmia. *Catalog: $2*

Lilypons Water Gardens
P.O. Box 10
6800 Lilypons Road
Buckeystown, MD
    21717-0010
Everything for the water garden,
    including animals. Catalog: $5

Mary's Plant Farm
2410 Lanes Mill Road
Hamilton, OH 45013
(513) 892-2055 or 894-0022
Native perennials, ferns, flowering
    shrubs and trees: shade-tolerant
    plants. Catalog: $1

McClure & Zimmerman
P.O. Box 368
108 West Winnebago
Friesland, WI 53935
(414) 326-4220

Netherlands importers, good quality.
    Catalog: free

Niche Gardens
1111 Dawson Road
Chapel Hill, NC 27516
(916) 967-0078
Nursery propagated natives, especially
    Southeast herbaceous plants, trees,
    and shrubs. Catalog: $3

Oak Hill Farm
204 Pressly Street
Clover, SC 29710
(803) 222-4245
Hardy evergreens, species rhododen-
    drons. Catalog: free

Oakridge Nurseries
P.O. Box 182
East Kingston, NH 03827
(603) 642-8227
Rescued plants and propagated natives.
    Catalog: free

Owens Farms
Route 3, Box 158-A
Curve-Nankipoo Road
Ripley, TN 38063
(901) 635-1588
Native deciduous hollies.
    Catalog: $2

Picadilly Farm
1971 Whippoorwill Road
Bishop, GA 30621
(706) 769-6516
Hosta, Helleborus.
   Catalog: $1

Plant Delight Nursery, Inc.
9241 Sauls Road
Raleigh, NC 27603
(919) 772-4794
*Conifers, flowering shrubs, herbaceous
   perennials, grasses, hostas.
   Catalog: $2*

Roslyn Nursery
211 Burrs Lane
Dix Hills, NY 11746
(516) 643-9347
*Extensive catalog of rare and familiar
   woody plants, rhododendrons,
   pieris, kalmias, azaleas.
   Catalog: $2*

Russell Graham
4030 Eagle Crest Road NW
Salem, OR 97304
(503) 362-1135
*Wonderful collection of ferns, shade
   plants, and bulbs.
   Catalog: $2*

Savory's Gardens, Inc.
5300 Whiting Avenue
Edina, MN 55439
(612) 941-8755

*Perennials, shade plants,
   Hemerocallis, hostas.
   Catalog: $2*

Schild Azalea Gardens and
   Nursery
1705 Longview Street
Hixson, TN 37343
(615) 842-9686
*Primarily azaleas from the southeast
   U.S. and Asia, also rhododendrons,
   kalmias. Catalog: $1*

Shady Oaks Nursery
112 Tenth Avenue SE
Waseca, MN 56093
(507) 835-5033
*Shrubs, herbaceous perennials, hostas,
   native plants, ferns, ground covers
   for shade. Catalog: $2.50*

Sherer, S., & Sons
104 Waterside Road
Northport, NY 11768
(516) 261-7432
*Complete supplies, colocasias and
   giant taros, third generation.
   Catalog: free*

Siskiyou Rare Plant Nursery
2825 Cummings Road
Medford, OR 97501
(503) 772-6846
*Dwarf conifers; dwarf shrubs and
   trees; alpine, rock, woodland
   plants; hardy ferns. Catalog: $2*

Stoecklein's Nursery
135 Critchlow Road
Renfrew, PA 16053
(412) 586-7882
Wildflowers, shade plants.
Catalog: $1

Sunlight Gardens
Route 1, Box 600-A
Andersonville, TN 37705
(615) 494-8237
Shade perennials.
Catalog: $2

Sunnybrook Farms Nursery
9448 Mayfield Road
Chesterland, OH 44026
(216) 729-7232
Herbs, perennials, ivies, and hostas.
Catalog: $2

Sunshine Farm and Gardens
Renick, WV 24966
(304) 497-3163
Very rare and exceptional plants;
call or write for list

Transplant Nursery
Parkertown Road
Lavonia, GA 30553
(404) 356-8947
Southeastern U.S. natives, rhododen-
drons, camellia, chiefly azaleas

Washington Evergreen Nursery
P.O. Box 388
Brooks Branch Road
Leicester, NC 28748
Dwarf kalmias, rhododendrons,
conifers. Catalog: $2

Waterford Gardens
74 East Allendale Road
Saddle River, NJ 07458
(201) 327-0721
Good color catalog, helpful people.
Catalog: $4

We-Du Nurseries
Route 5, Box 724
Marion, NC 28752
(704) 738-8300
Woodland plants. Catalog: $1

White Flower Farms
Route 63
Litchfield, CT 06759
(203) 567-0801
Wonderful catalog, great information.
Catalog: $5

Woodlanders, Inc.
1128 Colleton Avenue
Aiken, SC 29801
(803) 648-7522
Native trees and shrubs and some
herbaceous perennials. Catalog: free

Title page: white bleeding-heart (*Dicentra spectabilis*), dusty-miller (*Senecio cineraria* 'Silver Dust') and spirea (*Spiraea x Vanhouttii*).
Contents page (clockwise from top left): moss, *Astilbe,* and lady fern (*Athyrium filix-femina*); *Polygobum aubertii; Petasites japonicus;* double bloodroot (*Sanfuinaria canadensis* 'Multiplex'). **p.11**: *Dicentra eximia* and toothwort (*Dentaria diphylla*). **Ornamental Shrubs** chapter opener (clockwise from top left): *Polygonatum biflorum, hydrangea* and *variegated Daphne x Burkwoodii* 'Carol Mackie'; a *Rhododendron* cultivar; *Spiraea x Vanhouttii;* azalea; *Rhododendron* 'Purple Gem'; *Corylopsis spicata; Leucothoe fontanesiana* 'Girard's Rainbow'. **Perennials for Flowers** chapter opener (clockwise from top left): windflower (*Anemone blanda*); *Ajuga reptans* 'Burgundy Glow'; *Oxalis violacea; Arisaema sikokianum; Primula;* a tuberous begonia hybrid; *Sedum spectabile.* **Perennials for Foliage** chapter opener (clockwise from top left): *Epimedium; Hakonechloa macra* 'Aureola'; *Hosta; Marsilea mutica; Onoclea sensibilis;* begonia and coleus. **Ground Covers and Vines** chapter opener (clockwise from top left): *Hedera canariensis* 'Variegata' and H. *colchica* 'Variegata'; *Lonicera sempervirens* 'Sulphurea'; *Wisteria sinensis; Pulmonaria* and *Anemone; Alchemilla mollis;* moss; Kenilworth ivy (*Cymbalaria muralis*). **Appendix** opener (clockwise from top left): Japanese painted fern (*Athyrium nipponicum*) 'Pictum' (A. goeringianum) and *Galium; Primula; Doronicum caucasicum* and *Lamium maculatum* 'Beacon Silver'; *Corydalis cheilanthus;* ferns; center photo: a *Rhododendron* hybrid. **p. 115**: *Hosta* 'Blue Cadet' and H. 'Sum and Substance'. **p. 118**: Goldie's wood fern (*Dryopteris goldiana*). **p. 123**: *Clematis x jackmanii.* **p. 126**: tulips beneath European white birch trees (*Betula pendula*)

U.S. Plant Hardiness Zones: Approximate range of average annual minimum temperatures (F°): zone 1: below -50°; zone 2: -50° to -40°; zone 3: -40° to -30°; zone 4: -30° to -20°; zone 5: -20° to -10°; zone 6: -10° to 0°; zone 7: 0° to 10°; zone 8: 10° to 20°; zone 9: 20° to 30°; zone 10: 30° to 40°